ENGLISH Direct 1

John Foster
Keith West

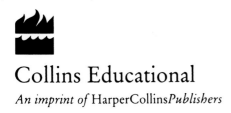

Collins Educational

An imprint of HarperCollins*Publishers*

Published by Collins Educational

An imprint of HarperCollins*Publishers* Ltd
77–85 Fulham Palace Road
London W6 8JB

First published 1998

ISBN 000 323 066 X

British Library Cataloguing in Publication Data.
A catalogue record for this book is available from the British Library.

Commissioned by Domenica de Rosa

Edited by Kim Richardson and Helen Clark

Picture research by Katie Anderson

Production by Susan Cashin

Design and layout by Ken Vail Graphic Design, Cambridge

Cover design by Ken Vail Graphic Design, Cambridge

Cover photographs: Getty Images and Telegraph Colour Library

Printed and Bound by Printing Express Ltd., Hong Kong.

Acknowledgements
The following permissions to reproduce material are gratefully acknowledged. Numbers refer to pages.

Illustrations
Argos Distributors Ltd. (6 top); Getty Images (6 bottom, 33, 35 all pictures, 37, 41, 42 top right & bottom right, 47, 52, 59, 76, 81, 95 middle & bottom); BBC (7, 88); John Walmsley (8, 13, 70, 71, 91, 93); © 20th Century Fox Corporation (10); *TV Quick* (11); London International Features Ltd., ©1995 Tri Star/Columbia, photo by Rob McEwan (14); Angus Mill (15, 16, 34 top, 44, 50 top); Judy Brown (18, 34 bottom, 58, 79, 84); Debbie Clark (20, 32, 38, 82); Clinton Banbury (21, 43, 53, 55, 72, 83, 89); Collins Educational (23); Sean Victory (24, 60, 61, 62); © Beulah Candappa (25); Cornwall Tourist Board (26); Tony Jarmain (27, 80, 86, 87); Alan Marks (28, 29, 30, 68, 69); Curtis Tappenden (31, 64, 65, 66); Benjamin-Taylor Associates (39); Telegraph Colour Library (42 top left & bottom left, 63, 78, 95 top); Harry Venning (54, 56 all pictures, 57, 77, 94); Alex Keene & Jo MacLennan (The Walking Camera) (67); Talk Radio (90); Rex Features Ltd. (92).

Text extracts
Stephanie Foulger's letter, from *The Young Telegraph*, 2 September 1995 (12); Adaptation of material from *TV Hits*, September 1996 (14); Extracts from *Classics from the Comics* No. 5, published by D. C. Thomson & Co Ltd, (17, 19); Extract from *No More Heroes* by David Clayton, published by Collins Educational (22); 'The Jumbie' is adapted from 'The Jumbie', in *Tales from the West Indies* by Faustin Charles, published by W. H. Allen & Co (24); 'Advice on storytelling' by Beulah Candappa (25); 'The Monkey's Paw', adapted by Keith West from 'The Monkey's Paw' by W. W. Jacobs; 'Smuggler's Cove', by Keith West (26); 'The Friendly Nurse', by Keith West (27); 'Abigail and Jack' by James Rigg – James Rigg is a pseudonym for John Foster and Keith West (28–29); 'The Face at the Window' is adapted from 'The Fleeing Corpse' by Mike Samuda, from *Ghosts* published by Edward Arnold (31); Extract from *Coming to England* by Floella Benjamin, published by Pavilion (39); *Sent Away from Home*, from *The Young Telegraph*, 9 September 1995 (40); Letters from *The Young Telegraph*, 9 September 1995, 17 August 1996 and 26 October 1996 (44–45); 'Snail', by Claire Pepperell (50); 'My Apple', by Rosalyn Low (50); 'Balloon', by Colleen Thibaudeau from *Madtail, Miniwhale and Other Shape Poems*, ed. Wes Magee, published by Viking (50); 'The Scarecrow', by Ruth West (51); 'Nouns' and 'Verbs' by Stuart Lewis – Stuart Lewis is a pseudonym for John Foster, (52–53); 'Mad Meals', by Michael Rosen, from *Quick, Let's Get Out of Here*, published by André Deutsch (53); 'Have you ever heard ...?' by John Foster © 1997 (54); Four limericks by Nick Timms (56–57); 'There was a pop singer called Fred', by Max Fatchen, from *Songs For My Dog and Other People*, published by Kestrel (57); 'Excuses, Excuses', by Gareth Owen, first published as 'Conversation Piece' in *Salford Road*, published by Fontana Lions (58); 'Song of the Victorian Mine', by Sue Cowling, from *What is a Kumquat?*, published by Faber and Faber (59); 'Anancy and Mongoose', adapted by Keith West from *Tales from the West Indies* by Faustin Charles, published by W. H. Allen & Co (60–61); 'Tiddalik the Flood-maker', adapted by John Foster from 'Tiddalik the Flood-maker' by C. P. Mountford, published by Rigby Ltd. (62–63); 'Daedalus and Icarus', adapted by Keith West (64–65); 'The Clever Servant', by Tony Mitton (66); 'Why Ganesh has an Elephant's Head' by Renuka Singh, from *Festivals* compiled by Jill Bennett, published by Scholastic, 1994 (67); 'Beowulf and Grendel' by John Foster and Keith West (68–69); 'Swimming Pools are Safer' and 'How to Phone for Help' are based on information from leaflets published by the Royal Life Saving Society UK (Tel: 01527 853943) (79, 82); 'Be Safe in the Saddle' by Eric Johnson – Eric Johnson is a pseudonym for John Foster (80); 'The Boy Who Boasted', by Charles Thomson (84–85); 'Nasim's First Day' is an adaptation by John Foster of an extract from page 8 of Berlie Doherty's novel *Tough Luck*, published by Collins Cascades (86–87); 'The Things From Out There' by Keith West (88); 'I say, I say, I say' contains extracts from *The Armada Book of Fun* compiled by Mary Danby, published by HarperCollins*Publishers* (92).

Contents

English Direct – Complete Coverage of the National Curriculum

English Direct 1 Year 7	English Direct 2 Year 8	English Direct 3 Year 9
Expressing Opinions 6 *Topics* TV programmes; Films and videos *Language focus* Sentences; Capital letters	**Expressing Opinions** *Topics* Pop shows; CDs; Book reviews *Language focus* Spelling	**Expressing Opinions** *Topics* Soaps; Cartoon comedies *Language focus* Paragraphs
Media Texts 16 *Topics* Comics; Graphic novels *Language focus* Exclamation marks; Spelling	**Media Texts** *Topic* Magazines *Language focus* IT skills	**Media Texts** *Topic* Newspapers *Language focus* IT skills
Storytelling 24 *Topic* Ghost stories *Language focus* Paragraphs; Plots	**Storytelling** *Topics* UFOs; Science-fiction stories *Language focus* Punctuation	**Storytelling** *Topic* Describing characters *Language focus* Grammar
Personal Writing 34 *Topic* Autobiography *Language focus* Drafting	**Personal Writing** *Topics* A class who's who; My life; Letter to a penfriend *Language focus* Capital letters and full stops; Letter writing; Verbs and tenses	**Personal Writing** *Topic* Diaries *Language focus* Spelling
Developing Arguments 42 *Topic* Letters to newspapers *Language focus* Drafting; Punctuation	**Developing Arguments** *Topics* Heroes and heroines; The school I'd like; Letters to newspapers *Language focus* Paragraphs; Conjunctions; Commas	**Developing Arguments** *Topics* How adults treat teenagers; Smoking *Language focus* Drafting and delivering speeches
Poetry 50 *Topics* Shape poems; List poems; Recipe poems; Limericks; Performance poems *Language focus* Nouns; Verbs	**Poetry** *Topics* Comparison poems *Language focus* Similes; Drafting	**Poetry** *Topic* Ballads *Language focus* Accent and dialect
Stories from the Past 60 *Topics* Myths and legends *Language focus* Library skills; Dictionary skills	**Stories from the Past** *Topics* The Canterbury Tales; An Indian folk tale; An American story and poem *Language focus* The development of the English language; Dictionary skills	**Stories from the Past** *Topics* Shakespeare's *Macbeth* *Language focus* The development of the English language; Dictionary skills
Conveying Information 70 *Topics* Messages and instructions; School rules; Class outings *Language focus* Letter writing; IT skills	**Conveying Information** *Topics* My hobby; Animal fact files; An A–Z of sports *Language focus* Drafting and delivering a talk	**Conveying Information** *Topics* Factsheets; Leaflets *Language focus* Sentences
Persuading 78 *Topics* Safety leaflets; Cautionary tales *Language focus* Spelling	**Persuading** *Topic* Advertising *Language focus* Adjectives; Spelling	**Persuading** *Topics* Brochures and leaflets *Language focus* Punctuation
Scripts and Scriptwriting 86 *Topics* Playscripts; Radio scripts *Language focus* Accents and dialects	**Scripts and Scriptwriting** *Topic* From script to stage *Language focus* Dialects	**Scripts and Scriptwriting** *Topic* From script to screen *Language focus* Register

The units Each unit looks at a particular way in which language is used. For example, in the first unit ('Expressing Opinions'), you will be looking at how language is used to express opinions. After seeing how other people have used language to express opinions, you will get the opportunity to practise expressing your own opinions about TV programmes, films and videos.

Each unit is divided into short chapters, which deal with different topics. For example, the first chapter in the book is called 'TV Programmes'.

The chapters also contain several different kinds of activity, which will help you to develop your basic skills in English. The boxes on the rest of this page tell you more about these activities, and give you some advice about how to do them.

To the Student

Speaking and Listening

There are a variety of speaking and listening activities, including story-telling, role-plays and making tape-recordings, as well as discussions. These will help you to develop your ability to speak confidently in various situations.

- Take turns to speak.
- Remember to listen carefully when others are speaking.
- When it is your turn, make sure you speak clearly.

Reading

You will be reading all kinds of material, such as short stories, play scripts, poems and letters. The reading activities will help you to develop your ability to read with understanding.

- Read the passages slowly and carefully.
- If you don't understand any words, don't give up: they may become clear later. (Or you can ask your teacher for help.)
- Look at the pictures: they may help you understand what is going on.

Writing

The writing activities will help you to learn how to express yourself well. You will be trying different kinds of writing, such as radio scripts, poems and accounts of personal experiences. You will also have the chance to design and draw picture-strips and posters, and to use the word processor.

- Think about the question or topic before you start writing.
- If you are answering questions on a passage in the book, look back over the passage carefully before you write.
- When you have finished, re-read what you have written, and correct any mistakes.

Other activities

- Several activities in this book will help you to improve your grammar, punctuation and spelling.
- Some units have activities that will help you use a library, find your way around a dictionary and practise using a word processor.
- Other activities include making sound effects for radio plays, interviewing people with different accents and performing a scene from a play.

In this unit you will be expressing your opinions about TV programmes. You will also be reading and writing reviews of films and videos.

TV Programmes

There are often arguments about what to watch on TV, because different people like different programmes. Here are some people talking about the programmes they like.

My mum likes news and documentaries. My dad likes romantic films.

Leanne

Greg

I like watching soaps. My favourites are *Home and Away* and *Brookside*.

My favourites are murder mysteries and horror stories.

Paul

The rest of the family are sports fans. I'd like to watch the wildlife programmes, but I never get the chance.

Maria

I enjoy comedy programmes and game shows.

Jasreen

Speaking and Listening

- In groups, discuss the types of programmes you like to watch, and explain why.

- Imagine you have to choose four favourite programmes. You can only choose one programme of each type. What is your favourite comedy? Your favourite soap? Your favourite cartoon? Your favourite game show?

In Pairs

Imagine you are in charge of a TV station called Channel Tomorrow, which broadcasts programmes at the weekend. Plan a full day's timetable for a Saturday. Start your day at 8 a.m. and go through until midnight. All your programmes must be new ones. Remember that people like different programmes, so plan to include a variety of different types of programme.

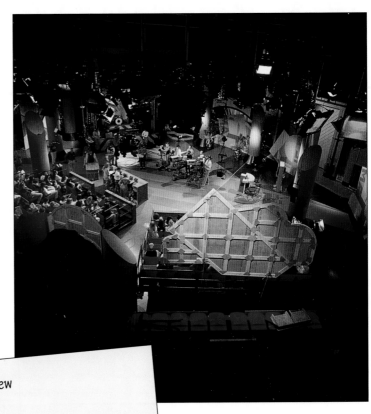

Here is the list of programmes that Suzanne and Paul planned.

8.00 a.m.	News and Sports Review
9.00 a.m.	Kiddies' Cartoons
10.00 a.m.	Mister Magic
10.30 a.m.	The New Planet – science fiction adventure
12.00 noon	Slush – magazine for teenagers
1.00 p.m.	News and Weather
2.00 p.m.	Sports Supreme – Tennis. Golf. Motor Sport. Wrestling. Results Round-up.
5.30 p.m.	Wonders of the Wild – animal programme
6.00 p.m.	Scampi Town – food programme
6.30 p.m.	Creek Bay – new soap – children in a seaside town
7.00 p.m.	Murder on Horseback – special film for TV
8.00 p.m.	Widow's Street – inner-city soap opera
9.00 p.m.	The Wild Beast of Crundale – Horror TV Special
11.00 p.m.	Football Galore
11.30 p.m.	Late News
12.00 p.m.	Close

My Favourite TV Programme

When you write, you must always write in **sentences**. If you do not use sentences, people will find it hard to understand what you have written.

- A **sentence** is something written or spoken that makes sense. It usually consists of several words.
- A sentence always begins with a **capital letter**.
- A sentence usually ends with a **full stop**, but it can also end with a **question mark** (?) or an **exclamation mark** (!).

Writing

- Write four or five sentences about your favourite TV programme. Start a new line each time you start a new sentence. Remember to begin and end each sentence properly.
- When you have finished, show your writing to a friend. Check that you have each used capital letters to begin your sentences and full stops to end them.

Here is what Tracy wrote about her favourite TV programme. She began each sentence on a new line. This helped her to remember to use a capital letter at the start of each sentence and a full stop at the end of each sentence.

> My favourite TV programme
> My favourite programme is EastEnders.
> I like it because there are lots of different characters.
> The stories are about people and their problems.
> It deals with important issues like selling drugs.
> Each episode leaves you wondering what will happen next.

On the right is what Tony wrote. It is hard to follow because he forgot to use capital letters and full stops.

Copy out what Tony has written. Put a capital letter at the start of each sentence and a full stop at the end of each sentence.

> my favourite programmes are the sports programmes i like all kinds of sports especially football programmes they are good because you get experts talking about the game there are interviews with the players and managers it helps you to understand what happened in the match

Capital Letters

Capital letters are used in several ways:

1 At the start of the first word in a sentence. For example:
This page is about using capital letters.

2 For the first letter of a person's name. For example:
Ajay Patel, Glenn Hoddle, Cindy Crawford.

3 For the first letter of the name of a place. For example:
Glasgow, Swansea, Birmingham.

4 For the first letter of a day of the week or of a month.
For example:
Monday, October.

5 For the word 'I'. For example:
My friend and I went to the shops.

6 For the first letter in the main words of titles of films,
books and TV programmes. For example:
*Top of the Pops, Home and Away, The Indian in the
Cupboard.*

7 For the first letter of the names of football teams and
bands. For example:
Newcastle United, Oasis.

8 For words used to show a person's title. For example:
Mrs Fowler, Sir Bobby Charlton, Prince Charles.

Writing

Copy out these sentences and correct them by putting in
capital letters.

1 my sister and i went to see michael jackson at wembley.

2 on thursday i watched neighbours and star trek.

3 gareth southgate missed a penalty for england against
germany.

4 the lead singer of blur is damon albarn.

5 in august shazia went to pakistan.

6 my mum is mrs simpson and my step-dad is mr walsh.

7 the part of joe is played by paul nicholls.

8 newcastle united paid £15 million for alan shearer.

9 naomi spotted lady thatcher at tescos on monday.

10 our dog is called bonzo and we live in willow road.

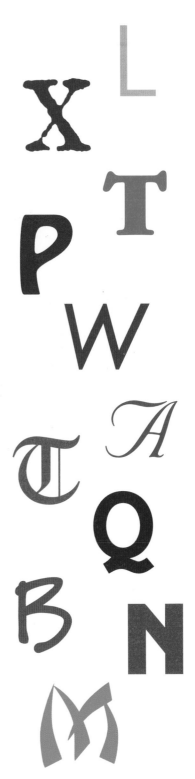

Pick of the Week

Magazines and TV guides often have an article about programmes that they think lots of people will want to watch. Here is an article suggesting some programmes that young people might want to watch.

STAR CHOICE!

Pick of the Week

The X Files (BBC1, 9.30 p.m.)

Don't miss the start of the new serial *The Demon Headmaster* (BBC 1, Wednesday, 4.35 p.m.), based on the book by award-winning author Gillian Cross. Later on Wednesday, there's another chance to see the stars falling over and forgetting their lines in a repeat of *Auntie's TV Bloomers* (BBC 1, 8.30 p.m.).

It's a bumper week for science fiction fans. Sunday afternoon's film on Channel 4 is *Kidnapped by Aliens* (2.15 p.m.). Then, Monday's episode of *U.F.O.* (BBC 2, 6.00 p.m.) has Foster's moon buggy struck by an alien craft. On Thursday, there are more strange happenings for Mulder and Scully to investigate in the first of a new series of *The X Files* (BBC 1, 9.30 p.m.). Finally, *Strange But True* (ITV, Friday, 9.00 p.m.) explores U.F.O. sightings in Britain and America.

This week also has plenty of animal programmes. You can choose between Channel 4's *Pet Patients* (Wednesday, 8.00 p.m.), which tells true stories from the Blue Cross animal hospital in London, and BBC's *Animal Hospital* (BBC 1, Thursday, 8.00 p.m.), which has Rolf Harris telling you how to rescue cats from treetops. Also on BBC 1, there's *Big Cat Diary* (Tuesday, 8.30 p.m.) about lions in Africa.

Saturday sees the return of *Casualty* (BBC 1, 8.05 p.m.) with an episode involving a joyriding accident, and there's an explosion at a fireworks factory in this week's *London's Burning* (ITV, Sunday, 9.00 p.m.). If it's real-life drama you want, then there's the rescue of four children from a smoke-filled house in *999 Lifesavers* (BBC 1, Tuesday, 8.00 p.m.).

Speaking and Listening

On your own, study the 'Pick of the Week' article on page 10 and choose one or two programmes that you would like to watch. Then, in groups, tell each other which programmes you chose and why.

Reading

Read the 'Pick of the Week' article and then answer these questions.

1 Which programme has an episode about a joyriding accident?

2 On which day can you watch a repeat of *Auntie's TV Bloomers*?

3 Which programme tells you how to rescue cats from treetops?

4 When can you watch a film called *Kidnapped by Aliens*?

5 Which series has an episode about an explosion in a fireworks factory?

6 Which programme is based on a book by Gillian Cross?

7 Which programme is about U.F.O. sightings in Britain and America?

8 On which channel is a new series of *The X Files* about to start?

9 Which programme tells true stories about the Blue Cross animal hospital?

10 When can you watch a programme about the rescue of four children trapped in a fire?

Writing

Find a newspaper or magazine that gives the TV programmes for either a day or a week. Select five or six programmes that you think people would like to watch. Then write your own 'Pick of the Day' or 'Pick of the Week' article.

Your article should include:

● the name of each programme;

● details of when it is on – the day, the TV channel and the time;

● something about the programme, for example, its content or its star.

Points of View

Here are some letters in which young people express their opinions about what they see on TV.

I'm really fed up with the way they show so much sport on TV. When there's something like the European Cup or the World Cup they show football on every channel. Last summer, there were the Olympics as well as the football, the cricket and the tennis. At one point there were no children's programmes on either BBC or ITV. Why can't they just record the sport and show it later on?

Thomas Sprindle

There is far too much news and weather on television. This Saturday there were eighty minutes of news and ten minutes of weather on the four channels.

You can get the news and weather from teletext and from newspapers. Why bore us by having so much news on television?

Besides, why is the news always so gloomy? It's all about wars and people dying in accidents. It's never about the good things that happen in the world.

Shaheena Aktar

Why do we have so many repeats on television and why are the repeats always of programmes that aren't worth watching?

I'm sick and tired of 'Dad's Army' with Arthur Lowe making a fool of himself. Also, 'Dad's Army' is repeated between 5 and 6 o'clock, at a time when children watch programmes. Yet the Second World War happened so long ago that 'Dad's Army' means nothing to us.

Martin Digsby

There seem to be lots of Australian programmes on TV and they're all very unrealistic. Take Neighbours, for instance. Most people in Ramsay Street seem to be related to each other, and horses are given as presents by friends and then everyone starts riding them around the street! This hardly happens in everyday life.

I'm glad Byker Grove is back. It's a good British programme that's funny, informing and, what's more, it's realistic. I wish there were more programmes like this on telly!

Stephanie Foulger

Speaking and Listening

Discuss the views that these four young people express (page 12). Do you agree or disagree with their views? Give your reasons.

1 Do you agree with what Stephanie says about Australian programmes?

2 Is there too much sport on TV?

3 Is there too much news and weather on TV?

4 Do you agree with Martin that there are too many repeats?

5 What sort of programmes would you like to see shown between 5 p.m. and 6 p.m.?

Writing

Write a letter in which you express your opinion either about a particular TV programme or about some of the programmes you see on TV. Remember to explain the reasons for your opinion and to write in sentences.

Speaking and Listening

Get into groups and read each other's letters.

Imagine you are planning a *Junior Points of View* programme in which you are going to read the letters.

● Choose someone to act as the presenter.

● Decide on the order in which you are going to read the letters.

● Then write a script for the presenter to read. The script should consist of one or two sentences to introduce each letter.

● When you are ready, practise your programme with each person reading their own letter.

● Then present your programme to the rest of the class.

Film and Video Reviews

A review of a film or a video is a piece of writing that tells you about the film or the video.

A good review should tell you three things:

- what sort of film it is;
- enough of the story for you to know what it is about;
- how good the film is and how much you are likely to enjoy it.

Here are some reviews from the magazine *TV Hits*.

reviews

LY/FILMS/VIDEO MS/VIDEOS/TELI EOS/TELLY/FILM

The Indian in the Cupboard
●●●○○

The title makes it sound a bit weird, but if you give this film a chance you're almost sure to enjoy it. The film is adapted from an award-winning novel by Lynne Reid Banks. It tells the story of Omri, a nine year old boy, who magically brings to life a three-inch high toy American Indian called Little Bear. Omri learns lots of important lessons about people and life from the wise old Indian.

A Little Princess
●●○○○

This is based on a book about a girl called Sara. She is sent to a strict boarding school when her dad is called to war. Before going to boarding school, Sara lived in the lap of luxury in India. She isn't very pleased about leaving it all behind, so she uses her imagination to create a snazzy life for herself. If you're into fairy stories, this one's for you!

Freaky Friday
●●●●○

This is a hilarious movie. It's about a mother and her thirteen year old daughter who swap places when they are magically transported into each other's bodies. Prepare to giggle yourself silly as Mum has to cope with biology classes and being sent to the headmistress. Meanwhile, her daughter, Annabelle, is faced with trying to save a sinking business.
It's a highly entertaining film based on the popular novel by Mary Rodgers.

Escape to Witch Mountain ●●●○○

One night a weird light shines from Witch Mountain and two baby twins are mysteriously found in a field. They are separated, but when they meet years later Danny and Anna feel a strange bond. They don't know why but they are drawn back to Witch Mountain. There's lots of spooky stuff as the twins find out that when they are together they have supernatural powers.

Jumanji
●●●●○

If you've seen the pictures of rhinos stampeding down the road and elephants treading casually over parked cars, then you'll know what to expect in this film. Robin Williams stars in the story of a boy who manages to get himself trapped inside a magical game for 26 years. When he is finally released, so are all the giant animals and evil powers that are part of the game! As you might have guessed, this causes a lot of confusion. A fabulous film!

Reading and Writing

Read the reviews, then write down the answers to these questions.

1 Which film is about a mother and daughter who change places?

2 In which film does a toy come to life?

3 In which film does a boy get trapped inside a game?

4 Which film is about a girl who is sent to a strict boarding school?

5 In which film are there giant animals?

6 Which film is about twins who get separated?

7 In which film does an adult get sent to the headteacher?

8 Which film is about a wise old man and a nine-year-old boy?

9 In which film do two children have supernatural powers?

10 Which three films are based on books?

Speaking and Listening

● The cover on a video is designed to make you want to watch it. Look at the covers on this page. In groups, say which you think is the best cover and why.

● On your own, design a cover for a new video called *The Night of the Beast*, about a prehistoric animal that comes to life. Then, in groups, discuss whose cover design is the best.

Writing

Choose a video that you have watched recently and write a review of it. Remember to say what sort of film it is, what the story is about and how good you think it is.

Comics

In this unit you will be looking at comics and graphic novels. You will learn about how stories are told in comic strips and graphic novels, and practise writing and drawing your own comic strips.

In a **comic**, stories are told in pictures as well as in words. The aim of popular comics like the *Beano* and the *Dandy* is to tell funny stories. Often, the humour is based on the fact that someone tries to do something naughty, but it goes wrong. The trick that they are playing misfires and they end up with people laughing at them instead.

Reading and Writing

Read the story of Beryl the Peril (page 17), then answer these questions. Make sure you write in sentences.

1 What is Beryl pretending to be at the start of the story?

2 What does Beryl's mum tell her to do?

3 How does Beryl get out of doing what her mum wants?

4 What does Beryl's dad find when he comes in?

5 Why does Beryl's dad go into the garden and start digging?

6 Why does Beryl start digging in the garden?

7 What does Beryl dig up?

8 Why are Beryl's mum and dad laughing at the end of the story?

Speaking and Listening

Carry out a survey to find out what people's favourite comics are. Ask people these questions:

● What is your favourite comic?

● Why is it your favourite comic?

● Which is your favourite comic character?

Keep a record of their answers. Then report your findings to the rest of the class in a class discussion.

Writing

Make a display of your favourite comics and your favourite comic characters to put on the wall. Write a comment beneath each item that you put on display. Your comment should consist of at least two sentences.

For example, you could begin the sentences like this:
This is my favourite comic because …
I think … is the funniest comic character because …

20

Features of Comic Strips

Here are some features that are typical of comic strips.

Speech and thought bubbles

In comic strips the words that people speak are put inside speech bubbles

The words that they think are put inside thought bubbles.

Capital letters

Often all of the words in a comic strip are written in capital letters, not just the first letter in a sentence or in a name. For example:

MUM SAW BILLY IN THE STREET.

Exclamation marks

Comic writers often use an exclamation mark at the end of a sentence, rather than a full stop.

● An exclamation mark is a punctuation mark which looks like this: !
● An exclamation mark shows that something dramatic is being said. For example:

QUICK! LET'S GET OUT OF HERE!

● An exclamation mark is also used when a command is being given. For example:

COME HERE AT ONCE!

Key words

A number of key words are used to show what is happening and how people are feeling. Here are some examples:

 UGH!

means how awful, how disgusting

 BIFF!

means a punch, a blow

 WHIZZ!

means moving very quickly

 GOLLY!

means surprise

 EEK!

means surprise or help!

 SOB!

means crying

Pictures and symbols

In addition to key words, pictures and symbols are used to show what is happening.

● A light-bulb above someone's head means that the person has an idea.

● A question mark above someone's head means that the person doesn't understand.
● Beads of sweat on a person's face mean that the person is very worried.

Speaking and Listening

Read 'Roger the Dodger's Dodge Clinic' (above).

- Talk about how Roger's dodge misfires, just as Beryl's trick did.
- What is Roger's dodge to stop his mum nagging him about how loud his music is?
- Why does the dodge backfire?

Writing

In pairs, study the list of features of comic strips (page 18). Now answer these questions.

- How many exclamation marks can you find in 'Roger the Dodger's Dodge Clinic'?
- Look at some other comic strips and find some more examples of the key words, pictures and symbols that are used in comics. Make a list of them and their meanings.

Writing and Drawing

1 Plan and then write and draw another story about Roger the Dodger, thinking up a dodge that backfires. Here are some situations that he could think up a dodge for:
   - Getting let off homework.
   - Being allowed to go home early.
   - Not doing the washing up.
   Either choose one of these situations or think up one of your own.

   When you have thought of his dodge, you need to think of how it backfires. Talk together in pairs or groups to help you to think of ways in which the dodge could backfire.

2 Imagine you have been asked to plan, write and draw a comic strip story for a new comic for children aged 7–11. Either invent a character of your own or tell a story about one of these people: Clumsy Clarissa, Messy Mitch, Dopey Daz or Magic Miranda.

Make Your Own Picture-strip

Here is an exciting horror story for you to turn into a picture-strip. First, read the story.

The Monkey's Paw

A poor old couple and their son are living happily together. One day, the old man's brother arrives. He is a colonel in the army and he has just come back from abroad. He shows the family a monkey's paw.

'The paw is magic,' he tells them. 'It can grant people three wishes, although it is evil.'

As the colonel is leaving, he throws the paw on the fire. The old man jumps forward and rescues the paw before it burns.

That night he can hardly sleep as he plans what he is going to wish for. Next day he makes a wish.

'Give me £5,000,' he asks the paw. It twists in his hands. Nothing happens until the following morning. Then someone comes to the house.

'Your son has been badly mangled in a machine at work. He is dead. But you will receive £5,000 from the factory owners as compensation for your son's death.'

After a few days, the couple make another wish. 'We want our son back with us,' they both say.

That night they hear a dragging sound as if someone is coming up the path. Then there is a knock on the door. They open it to find their son. He has returned from the grave covered in the wounds he received from his accident.

As soon as he sees his son, the old man grabs the monkey's paw. He makes a final wish. 'I want my son to return to his grave,' he cries.

The couple realise that the paw only brings evil. They go across to the fireplace and throw the paw in the fire.

Writing and Drawing

Turn the story of the monkey's paw into a picture-strip.

- First, plan how many pictures you are going to need.
- Once you have worked out how many pictures you are going to need, draw that number of boxes on a large sheet of paper.
- Prepare your picture-strip. Do not worry if you cannot draw very well. You can either just draw stick people or write a brief description of what the picture would show.

Here is how Leanne started her picture-strip.

Spelling

Letter Patterns

When you write, it is important to spell each word correctly. If you do not spell the words correctly, people can find it hard to understand what you have written.

One way you can help yourself to improve your spelling is by learning to notice letter patterns at the beginning and ends of words. Here is a table showing some common patterns of letters that occur at the beginning of words:

Letter pattern	Examples
bl	blow, blood
br	brick, brown
ch	chin, chair
cl	clap, clean
cr	crow, crash
dr	drop, drain
fl	flower, flag
gl	glass, glare
pl	play, plum
pr	pram, prize
sh	ship, shark
sl	slim, slide
sn	snip, sneeze
sp	spin, space
st	steam, stage
tr	trip, trunk

In Pairs

Work together to write lists of other words that begin with these letter patterns. Then use a dictionary to check the spellings of the words that you have added to the list.

How to Learn your Spellings

Keep a spelling book. When your teacher shows you that you have made a mistake, write the correct spelling of the word in your spelling book. Then use this method to learn it:

1 LOOK at the whole word carefully.
2 FOCUS on the part of the word that you got wrong.
3 SAY the word out loud.
4 COVER the word.
5 WRITE the word out without looking at it.
6 CHECK to see that you have spelt it correctly.

If you keep on getting it wrong, ask your teacher to help you find a way of remembering the tricky part of the word.

Shivering shellfish, I've been shipwrecked by a shark!

Graphic Novels

There are some books that look like comics because they tell the story through pictures as well as words. These books are called **graphic novels**. Here is the start of a graphic novel called *No More Heroes* by David Clayton. In the book, Nick Dale has a dream about his dad, because he has not seen him for a long time.

Chapter 1
Man on a Spider

Far out in the North Sea, Nick Dale's dad was working high up on the oil rig that stood, like a giant spider, against the moon.

It had been a quiet night so far. But now danger ran like sparks through the boy's body as he watched his dad work.

... and then came the roar.

A minute before, the sea had been a sheet of silver steel. Now, a giant shadow ran across it.

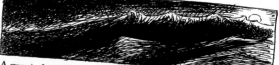

A great, dark wave, over a hundred metres high, raced like an express train towards the rig.

Up and up, on and on, it came, its foamy fingers snatching at the air.

Dad, look out!

But the oil men did not move. Suddenly, the wave was upon them. Billions of tons of water blotted out the moon like a great, black ghost.

Speaking and Listening

In groups, discuss what you think might happen next. Make a note of all your suggestions, then share your ideas in a class discussion.

Writing and Drawing

Plan and then write and draw the first chapter of a graphic novel called *The Nightmare*. Make it as exciting and dramatic as you can. You only have to do the first chapter, so you don't have to work out how the story ends. Don't worry if you cannot draw very well, just draw stick people. It's the ideas that count, not the drawings!

When you have finished, show each other what you have done and share ideas about how the story could go on.

Reading

You can read the rest of David Clayton's story in the book *No More Heroes* in the Collins Comets series. Here is a selection of the other titles in the Comets series. Choose one of them, read it and then tell the rest of the class what it is about and what you liked or disliked about it.

- *Time Exchange* by Jon Blake
- *Beware the Elvis Man* by David Clayton
- *Hell-Ride Tonight* by David Clayton
- *The Great Safe Blag* by Jean Ure and Leonard Gregory
- *The Tornado* by S.B.V. Moody
- *Exterminators 2 – Humans 0* by Ian Gregory
- *Suzuki, Goodbye* by Sam McBratney
- *The Soldier Who Never Was* by Mick Gowar
- *Sir Gawain and the Rugby Sevens* by Mick Gowar

In this unit you will be looking at ghost stories. As well as reading ghost stories, you will have a chance to tell and write your own ghost stories.

Ghost stories are told all round the world. This story comes from the West Indian island of Dominica, where the ghost or spirit of a dead person is called a jumbie. A jumbie is a spirit who cannot rest in peace.

The Jumbie

The Jumbie

Serena Fortune had fallen in love with a boy called Louis Baptiste. Louis only met Serena at night and nobody knew where he came from.

Serena's mother began to worry. 'Any time you ask him about coming to lunch or something like that, he always make an excuse.'

Her father decided to find out where Louis lived. He followed Louis home, but he seemed to disappear into the ruins of a burned out house.

Mr Fortune was sure Louis was a jumbie. He was hurrying home to tell his wife and Serena when he suddenly felt a sharp pain in his chest. He collapsed and died from a heart attack.

At Mr Fortune's funeral, an old woman came up to Mrs Fortune. She told her that Louis and all his family had died when their house was burned down five years ago. Louis Baptiste was a jumbie.

When Louis Baptiste next visited Serena, her mother picked up a Bible and held it out towards him. At once, Louis changed into smoke and the smoke drifted from the house and up into the moonlit sky.

Reading and Speaking

Read 'The Jumbie' and make a list of the main events in the story. Then take it in turns to retell the story, without looking at either the book or the list of events.

Speaking and Listening

- In groups, think about ghost stories you have heard. What tales are there about local ghosts? What ghost stories you have read or seen on TV?

- Read what Beulah Candappa says on page 25 about how to tell a story, and then take it in turns to tell each other a ghost story. Discuss who made their story most exciting because of the way they told it, and choose one person from your group to tell their story to the whole class.

Telling Ghost Stories

Beulah Candappa is a storyteller. Here she is talking about ways of getting your listeners interested in the story and making your story exciting.

> Shhh … Let me share my secrets … Sit close together in a 'magic circle'. Dim the lights. Then …
>
> Tell your story as if it actually happened to *you*, or someone you know. Breathe the fire of life into your story. Tell it as if *you* are *there*.
>
> Begin in a dramatic way. As you tell the story, make it so interesting that your listeners keep wondering: 'What happens next?' Use colourful language to *paint* the story for your audience, and build up to a dramatic ending.
>
> When you begin, let your eyes move slowly over your audience, and keep eye contact all through the story. Use your hands and your face to express feelings.
>
> Above all, use your voice. Change its pace and volume. Let it rise and fall. Don't forget to pause for dramatic effect. And make sure you can be heard!
>
> Here is an example from a scary story:
>
> *Silence … Suddenly … 'HUH!' … (dramatic pause) … 'Whar-oomph!' … Something slimy and slithery swooshed past them. There was a rattle of chains, and then they heard … (dramatic pause) … a hideous cackling, 'Hee-hee-hee-hee!'*

Speaking and Listening

- In pairs, make up a ghost story about two children who go exploring a ruined building and find that it is haunted. Practise telling each other the story, then join up with another pair and take it in turns to tell each other your stories.

- Get into groups. You have been asked to make a tape-recording of some ghost stories for a radio programme to be broadcast on Hallowe'en. In addition to each of you telling a ghost story, you could include some other items. For example, you could read an extract from a ghost story, or a poem that tells a ghost story. In pairs, you could also role-play interviews with people who say they have seen a ghost.

  When you have decided what to include, write out a plan of your programme and choose someone to act as the presenter who will introduce each item. When you have made your programme, take it in turns to play it to the rest of the class.

Recognising Paragraphs

Read the ghost story below. Notice how it is divided into six parts.

Smuggler's Cove

About a hundred years ago, a young woman named Hannah fell in love with a smuggler. His name was Jake, and he hid all the smuggled goods in a cave near the sea in a place called Broadhaven. He said to Hannah, 'When I am rich, I will marry you.'

Each night, Hannah sneaked down to the cave with a candle in her hand and waited for Jake's boat to return.

One night there was a terrible storm. Hannah watched from the cave as her lover's boat was sinking beneath the powerful waves. She ran to the water's edge and watched Jake's boat breaking up on the rocks. She knew he would be drowned. 'My poor Jake, you will die,' she cried.

For the rest of her life, Hannah could be seen at night, walking down to the cave to meet the ghost of her lover secretly. She lived until she was an old lady.

If you walk at night to Smuggler's Cove, you might see a ghostly woman with a candle in her hand waiting for her lover.

You might see Jake, too!

What is a paragraph?

A **paragraph** is a group of sentences, all of which are about the same idea or subject.

Why do writers use paragraphs?

To show their readers that they are going to write about another idea or subject. In a story, they start a new paragraph when they start to describe another incident in the story.

How do you know where a new paragraph begins?

Writers do three things to show where a new paragraph starts:

1 They start the first sentence of a new paragraph on a new line.
2 They leave a space between the margin (the edge of the page) and the first word of a new paragraph.
3 They often leave a blank line, known as a line space, between paragraphs.

Here is another ghost story. Look carefully at the way it is divided into paragraphs.

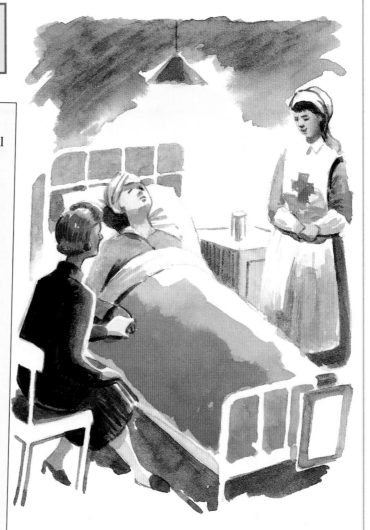

The Friendly Nurse

A man was lying seriously ill in a hospital in Glasgow. It was in 1942, during the Second World War. The man was called George McGeever. He had stepped on a German bomb in France. The bomb had exploded. Everyone thought that George McGeever was dying.

His wife Ethel McGeever was sitting beside his bed. Mrs McGeever refused to believe that he was dying. For two nights and two days she sat there, holding his hand. Although she was tired, she wouldn't let herself sleep. She felt that as long as she stayed awake, her husband would stay alive.

During the third night, a nurse in a strange uniform entered the room. She told Mrs McGeever that she could go to sleep now. The danger had passed. Her husband would get better. At once, Mrs McGeever fell fast asleep.

Later, another nurse shook Mrs McGeever and woke her up. She told Mrs McGeever that her husband was better and wanted to speak to her. Mrs McGeever told this nurse about the friendly nurse in the odd uniform who had told her she could go to sleep. The nurse who had woken her up smiled and said Mrs McGeever must have been dreaming. No one nowadays wore uniforms like the one Mrs McGeever had described. That was the sort of uniform a nurse would have worn in 1918 during the First World War. The friendly nurse was a ghost!

Reading and Writing

Read the story above, which consists of four paragraphs. Then write answers to these questions:

1 The first paragraph introduces the story.
  (a) Where does the story take place?
  (b) When does it take place?
  (c) Who is this paragraph about?
  (d) What does it tell you about him?

2 (a) Who is the second paragraph about?
  (b) What does it tell you about her and what she is doing?

3 What happens in the third paragraph?

4 What happens in the fourth paragraph?

Abigail and Jack

1 It happened nearly two hundred years ago. But in the village they still tell the tale of Abigail and Jack. Abigail was a fair, slim girl with pale blue eyes. Jack was a strong, handsome and well-built young man. He was eighteen, but Abigail was only fourteen.

2 They often met in secret in the churchyard, where they sat on a bench talking and kissing. They wanted to marry, but Jack worked on Abigail's father's farm. Abigail's father wanted her to marry a nobleman, not a farm labourer.

3 One day, while they were sitting in the churchyard, they heard a gravedigger singing. He sang about death and how everyone dies – the rich man, the poor man, the beggar man, the thief. He worked as he sang, using his shovel to dig a new grave. Jack and Abigail listened to his song. He sang that everyone must die. Only love can conquer death. His singing gave Abigail and Jack hope. They made up their minds. Jack would ask her father to allow them to marry.

4 But when Jack spoke to Abigail's father, he flew into a rage. He said he would never allow his daughter to marry a common labourer. He told Jack that he was dismissed and that he must leave the village. Then he sent for Abigail. He told her that she must go and pack. He was sending her to a boarding school.

5 Jack left the village that night. He wandered the countryside looking for work. But every farm he called at turned him away. Abigail's father had made sure that no one would employ him. As the weeks passed, he grew ill. He made his way back to the village, but within three days he was dead.

6 Meanwhile, at her boarding school, Abigail cried herself to sleep each night. There was no word from Jack. Surely he could not have forgotten her?

7 Then, one night in December, she awoke to find Jack standing beside her bed. His finger was on his lips to tell her not to speak. Thinking her father must have sent for her, she dressed quickly and hurried outside.

8 There in the driveway was Abigail's father's horse and carriage. Abigail climbed up beside Jack. She watched him as he drove them towards her home. He was still and silent. She felt his hands, which were as cold as ice. She gave him her gloves. She touched his cheeks. They too felt like ice. She gave him her scarf. He still looked cold. So she wrapped her coat around him.

9 When they reached the farm, it was in darkness. Abigail was surprised that neither her father nor the servants were up. Surely, they couldn't have all gone to bed, when they knew she was coming. She went and knocked on her father's door. Her father was surprised to see her. When she told him that Jack had brought her home, his face grew angry. He told her not to be so stupid. Jack was dead. Abigail fell to the floor in a faint.

10 When she came round, her father lit lanterns and took her to the graveyard. He wanted to show her Jack's grave and prove to her that he was dead. But when they reached the grave, Abigail had another shock. There on top of the grave were her gloves, her scarf and her coat.

11 Abigail never recovered from Jack's death. Within six months, she too was dead. Her last request was to be buried beside Jack.

12 If you visit the churchyard, you can still see their graves. From Jack's grave there grows a bright red rose. From Abigail's grave there grows a pure white rose. The two roses have grown towards each other and are tangled together.

James Rigg

Reading and Writing

Read the story of Abigail and Jack, which has twelve paragraphs. Then write sentences in answer to these questions. There is one question on each paragraph.

1 State three things you learn about (a) Abigail, and (b) Jack. *(paragraph 1)*

2 Why didn't Abigail's father want her to marry Jack? *(paragraph 2)*

3 What made Jack decide to speak to Abigail's father? *(paragraph 3)*

4 What happened when Jack spoke to Abigail's father? *(paragraph 4)*

5 Why do you think Jack grew ill and died? *(paragraph 5)*

6 Why did Abigail cry herself to sleep each night? *(paragraph 6)*

7 What did Abigail think when she woke up to find Jack at her bedside? *(paragraph 7)*

8 (a) How did Jack behave on the journey home?
(b) What three things did Abigail give him? *(paragraph 8)*

9 (a) What surprised Abigail when she got to the farm?
(b) Why did Abigail faint? *(paragraph 9)*

10 What did Abigail find in the graveyard? *(paragraph 10)*

11 Why did Abigail die and where was she buried? *(paragraph 11)*

12 What will you see if you visit their graves? *(paragraph 12)*

Writing

Imagine that Abigail kept a secret diary, which was found only after her death. Below is an example of an entry she might have written. Read it, then write some more of her diary entries.

April 20th

I have met a handsome young man named Jack. The problem is, I know my father won't approve. Jack is a farm labourer, and Father wants me to marry a noble — perhaps the King's younger son. Jack and I meet in secret by the graveyard.

The Face at the Window

The scream echoed through the house. Edward Cranswell snatched up his loaded pistol and ran down the dark corridor. He knew exactly what he had to do. The madman had attacked his brother once before. He was going to cut off the lunatic's escape. While Edward ran to the garden, his sister Amelia burst into their brother's room. He was still screaming. He pointed towards the window. Pressed against the glass was the most hideous face she had ever seen. A thin brown hand was fumbling with the window catch. But for a second Amelia was unable to move. The man's eyes seemed to hold her spellbound. They bored into her, daring her to go closer. As Amelia raised her pistol to fire, the man snarled. Then, he turned and fled. Michael was too frightened even to speak. He collapsed on Amelia's shoulder and started to sob. He remembered the dreadful night when the man first broke into his room. He saw again the face with the scar, the twisted mouth and the long grey hair.

Reading and Discussion

Above is the start of another ghost story. But the writer has forgotten to show where the paragraphs begin. Read it through and decide where you think the new paragraphs should begin.

Then, in groups, compare your views.

Writing a Ghost Story

The plot

Every story has a **plot**. The plot is the outline of the series of events that happen in the story. Often you can sum up the plot of a story in a few sentences, or show it in the form of a flow chart.

On the right is a flow chart showing the plot of the story of Abigail and Jack, which you read on pages 28 and 29.

Another way of planning a plot is to draw a **storyboard**. A storyboard is a series of pictures which show the main events of the plot. Below is the start of a storyboard showing the main events of the story of Abigail and Jack.

Abigail, a rich farmer's daughter, falls in love with Jack, a farm labourer.

⬇

Abigail's father won't let them marry.

⬇

Jack is dismissed and leaves the village.

⬇

Abigail is sent to boarding school.

⬇

Jack dies and his ghost comes to take Abigail home.

⬇

Abigail dies of a broken heart and is buried next to Jack.

Abigail and Jack met secretly in the churchyard.

Abigail's father refused to let her marry Jack.

One day they heard a gravedigger singing about love and death.

Speaking and Listening

In pairs, discuss what the rest of the storyboard would show.

Here are some entries from an *A–Z of Ghosts and Hauntings*. Each one tells you about a place that is haunted and a ghost that haunts it.

20 A–Z of Ghosts and Hauntings

Farnham Wood

Several places in and around Farnham Wood are said to be haunted by a beautiful young woman called Kate, dressed in brown. If you go into the wood and she calls you, do not turn around. If Kate stares into your eyes, she turns into a little girl and you become old and ill.

Hawkford

The old road from Hawkford to Hurlston is haunted by a man driving a ghostly horse-drawn carriage. The man has no head. This is the ghost of Charlie Gardiner, who has been spotted many times on the old road.

In 1864 Charlie fell in love with Elizabeth Broughton, a local beauty. Her father, Squire Broughton, did not like Charlie. He found out that Charlie and his daughter

A–Z of Ghosts and Hauntings 21

were planning to run away together. When Charlie arrived in his carriage, Squire Broughton was waiting for him with his axe. Ever since, people have reported seeing the headless driver and the ghostly carriage fleeing from Hawkford Manor.

Helton

People in Helton say the town is haunted by a strange black cat. It is twice the size of a normal cat. Anyone who sees it is said to fall under the spell of its hypnotic green eyes. It leads them out into the marshes, where they fall into the peat bog and drown. The cat is said to be the ghost of Benjamin Waters's old tom-cat. Benjamin was a farmer who died when he fell into the peat bog in 1876. His cat escaped but was killed by the local people, who thought it had brought Benjamin bad luck. They say that it has come back to get its revenge.

Houndsbury

An old man is sometimes seen at Houndsbury Park around midnight. He wears a long black coat and leans heavily on a thick walking stick. His hair is long and white. He beckons people towards him with his stick. If you go to him, you find yourself looking into the face of a grinning skull. He then vanishes. But it's best to keep away from him. Everyone who has seen the grinning skull has died a few weeks later in a strange accident.

Reading, Speaking and Listening

- In pairs, read the entries from the *A–Z of Ghosts and Hauntings*. Choose one of them which you think would make a good basis for a ghost story.
- Work out the plot for a story involving a boy or girl who visits the place and sees the ghost. Then, one of you draw a flow chart listing the main events in your plot, while the other draws a storyboard of the plot.
- Which shows your plot more clearly – the flow chart or the storyboard?

Writing

Write your own ghost story. Before you begin, plan it by making a flow chart or drawing a storyboard of the plot.

Then, write your story. Remember to divide your story into paragraphs, and use your flow chart or storyboard to help you to decide when you need to start new paragraphs.

In this unit you will be talking and writing about yourself and your life. You will also be reading about some other people's lives.

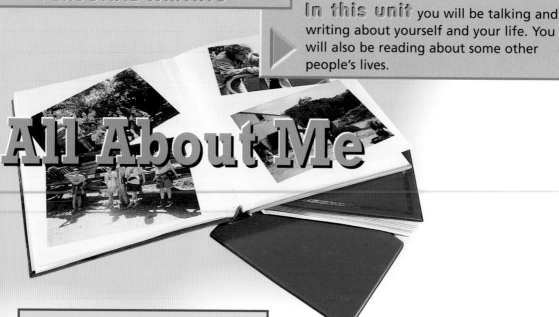

All About Me

Here is Leanne talking about herself.

I am a 12-year-old girl called Leanne. I live with my mum and three brothers in a two-storey terraced house. My brothers are called Mark, Kevin and Jamie. They are all older than me.

We have two pets – a big bloodhound dog called Bill and a ginger rabbit called Suzie. Bill needs plenty of exercise, and I take him for a walk every morning before school. Suzie stays in her hutch.

I like making new friends and I hate school dinners. Mum makes sandwiches for me. My favourite sandwiches are cheese and tomato.

The funniest thing that happened to my brother Mark was when he went into the garage to look for a screwdriver. He banged his head on one of the shelves and a can of oil fell into his hair. Mum and I laughed, but he was angry. The oil dripped down his neck and splashed on the front of his new shirt.

At the comprehensive school, which I have just joined, I am in the swimming club. I am the fastest swimmer in my class.

Speaking and Listening

1 Working in pairs, discuss what you have learned about:
   (a) Leanne's family
   (b) her pets
   (c) her likes and dislikes
   (d) a funny event in her life
   (e) her hobbies.

2 Imagine your partner knows nothing about you. Take it in turns to tell them all about yourself, in the way that Leanne has told us all about herself.

Something I'll Never Forget

Here are some other children writing about things they will never forget.

My dad died when I was only eight years old. I stayed with my gran and grandad for quite a while until Mum got over the shock. Things are fine now. I have a stepdad, and he takes me to football matches. I wear all the latest football clothes and I listen to the latest music on my new CD player. But I sometimes wonder what my dad would say if he could see me now!

Paul

Mum tried to teach me to swim when I was very young. I held her hand and she paddled out to sea with me. A big wave separated us and I remember sinking, and salty water in my mouth. Dad came to the rescue, but I've been afraid of the water ever since.

Suzanne

We once had a black Labrador called Sooty. She ran out of our front gate and onto the main road. She was run over by a large van. She died instantly. My Mum cried and I hugged her.

Cassie

When I was nine, my dad told me we were going to visit my cousins in Birmingham. We arrived at the station in London — I can't remember which station now — and we got on a big train. It was so long, it looked like a giant snake.

I expected the weather to be hot in Birmingham, but when we walked outside the station it was raining. My uncle was waiting for us. My dad carried the cases, but he dropped them all when he saw his brother. They gave each other a gigantic hug. My cousins seemed to be shy, and they laughed when I spoke. They thought my accent was funny, but I couldn't understand them when they spoke with a Birmingham accent.

My uncle took us all to his house. My dad was surprised to find that my grandparents had flown in from India. This was the best moment of my life!

Nozrul

Writing

Did any of these stories remind you of something that happened to you? Think of an incident that you'll never forget, because it was an exciting or important moment in your life. Write a few sentences about it in the way that these children have done.

Remember to start each sentence with a capital letter and to end it with a full stop. Before you hand in your writing, ask someone else to help you to check that you have put in all the capital letters and full stops.

The Story of My Life

Writing your life story is called writing an **autobiography**.

The story of your whole life would be very long, so you will have to decide what you are going to put in. The best thing to do is to choose the interesting parts and leave out the dull bits.

When you do a piece of writing, you should do it in five stages. Here is a diagram of the five stages:

Stage 1 Collecting ideas	Stage 2 Making a plan and writing the first draft	Stage 3 Revising and redrafting	Stage 4 Checking the grammar, punctuation and spelling	Stage 5 Writing or printing a neat copy

Follow these five stages as you write your life story.

Stage 1: Collecting ideas

What are the things about yourself that other people would find interesting? Here are some suggestions:

*My earliest memories
*Where I live   *My family
*Our pets *Things I like/dislike
*My hobbies and interests
*Funny events   *Sad events
*Exciting events.

In your exercise book, make some notes of things that you are going to put in your life story. Show your ideas to a friend or to someone in your family. Ask them if they think you have left anything important out.

Stage 2: Making a plan and writing the first draft

Look at your notes and make a plan of the order in which you are going to write about your life story. Think about how you are going to start. You need to make your first sentence as exciting as possible. Here are examples of how some children have started their life stories:

"The funniest thing that's happened was the day my dad tore his trousers."

"I can't remember much about when I was a baby."

"There are only two people in my family — me and my mum."

Choose how you are going to begin, then start writing your first draft.

A **draft** is a piece of writing that you are working on. It's a bit like a practice. You change a draft to improve it, until it says exactly what you want.

Stage 3:
Revising and redrafting

Paul decided to start the story of his life by writing about the time they had a car accident. Here is his first draft:

> I remember the time we had an accident. We were on our way to the seaside. Dad overtook a car and we swerved into a ditch. My sister hurt her head and Mum had a nosebleed. Dad got very angry. We never got to the seaside.

Paul showed his first draft to Kermal, who asked Paul some questions and suggested he put in more details.

66 I wondered which seaside town they were going to and what they planned to do. I was puzzled to know why Paul's dad had to swerve into a ditch. I wanted to know if his sister was badly hurt and why his dad was angry. I said I thought he could put in lots more details. 99

Here is Paul's second draft:

> ### The Accident
> It was my sister's ninth birthday. We were on our way to Blackpool to go to the fun fair and go on the pier. My dad pulled out to overtake another car. There was a big lorry coming towards us. Dad swerved to avoid it and we ended up in a ditch.
>
> Our car turned upside down and my sister cut her forehead. Mum bumped her nose, which started to bleed. There was blood everywhere. Dad was shouting and swearing because the car was so badly damaged.
>
> An ambulance came and took us all to hospital. My sister had to have six stitches. We never got to the seaside.

In Pairs

- List all the extra details that Paul has put in his second draft, which are not in his first draft.
- Take it in turns to show each other your first drafts. Ask each other questions in the way that Kermal asked Paul questions. Suggest some changes your partner could make, in order to explain what happened more clearly and to make it more interesting by putting in more details.
- Then write your second drafts.

Stage 4: Checking the grammar, punctuation and spelling

When you have finished your second draft, you need to read it through to check for any mistakes. Your teacher or a partner can help you to do this by reading it through and marking any mistakes in pencil.

Jack's teacher read through his work and pointed out some mistakes in his grammar:

We was running across the park when we hears this shout, I turns round to see whose there and I sees this man chasing after us. We was really scared, he was shouting at us and there wasn't nowhere for us to hide.

In groups, discuss Jack's mistakes and how to correct them. Then, on your own, copy out what Jack wrote and correct the mistakes.

Priya looked at Leanne's work and pointed out some spelling mistakes:

In the resent swimming contest I came first in the bak strok and third in the front craul rase.

In pairs, choose the correct spellings from those listed below. Then copy out the sentence, correcting the spelling mistakes.

recent   bake   stroak   crawl   raze

recant   back   stroke   cruel   race

In Pairs

Show each other your second drafts. Read through them to check for grammar, punctuation and spelling mistakes. Mark any mistakes in pencil and then give the draft back to your partner to do any corrections.

Stage 5:
Writing or printing a neat copy

Now that you have redrafted and checked your writing, you are ready to produce your final draft. Paul's class decided to put their life stories on display for an open evening, so he typed his story on a word processor and printed out two copies. He put one on display and took the other home for his family to read.

The Accident

It was my sister's ninth birthday. We were on our way to Blackpool to go to the fun fair and go on the pier. My dad pulled out to overtake another car. There was a big lorry coming towards us. Dad swerved to avoid it and we ended up in a ditch.

Coming to England

The TV star Floella Benjamin came to Britain from the West Indian island of Trinidad in 1960. You can read the story of her childhood in her book *Coming to England*.

In this extract, she describes her feelings as she, her sister and her two brothers are about to board the ship to take them to England to join their parents.

Coming to England

Finally the day for our journey across the ocean came. My mother had asked her sister Olive to buy the tickets for all four of us. Auntie Olive lived in Port of Spain which was where we had to board the ship for England. We spent our final night with her before being packed into her car for the drive through the busy evening traffic to the port. I had been there before to wave goodbye to Dardie when he left the country. But now it was my turn to leave these tropical shores for the first time in my life. I was just about to begin a journey of a lifetime which would take fifteen days across 4,000 miles of ocean.

The excitement at the port gave me a tingle inside. I felt butterflies in my tummy. I could see the big ship far out in the water. It couldn't come right up

to the side of the wharf because the water wasn't deep enough, so everyone had to be transported to the ship in small motor boats. There was so much noise it was deafening, everyone was pushing and shoving, people were shouting, making sure their trunks and suitcases were safe as the boats

ferried backwards and forwards. I felt bewildered, lost amongst the other passengers and those who had come to bid them farewell. Many were hugging and crying as they said goodbye. Prayers were being said for a safe passage. Suddenly I started to cry too. I felt scared, but of what I wasn't sure. Perhaps it was because I now realized what was about to happen. I was leaving my homeland, the land where I had experienced great happiness with my family. Maybe it was because I was frightened of going into the small boat as it bobbed on the dark, oily water – water which crazily reflected the harbour lights like a liquid mirror and separated us from the waiting ship that seemed to be calling me to her. Maybe I was just scared of facing the unknown. I still don't know.

Reading, Speaking and Listening

Read Floella Benjamin's account of her feelings as she was about to go on board the ship.

In groups:

- Talk about how Floella felt, and why she started to cry.
- Talk about times when you have felt confused and scared, because you were going to do something new.

Writing

Write about a time when you have felt butterflies in your stomach. Explain where you were, what you were going to do and why you felt as you did.

Other People's Stories

Sent Away From Home

Imagine if you were sent to live in a different part of the country, and you were without your mum and dad. That's what happened to children during World War Two when they were evacuated (sent away from areas being bombed).

During the first three days of September 1939, more than 1.5 million children and mothers were taken from towns and cities into the country. For some, it was a great adventure, but being separated from your family is always tough. And for others the experience became a nightmare they would rather forget …

CASE HISTORY
Maisie Seager, 67

Maisie was evacuated from London to Wiltshire when she was 10.

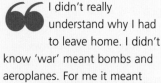

"I didn't really understand why I had to leave home. I didn't know 'war' meant bombs and aeroplanes. For me it meant leaving my mum and dad and my cat.

"I travelled to the country by train with my little sister and some other children from my school. When we arrived we were taken to the village hall and people came to look at us. It was like a cattle market. People said 'I'll have that one,' or 'I don't fancy that!'

"We were very lucky because we went to live with a woman who looked after us wonderfully. I learned how to knit and made scarves for the soldiers. Doing little chores stopped me feeling homesick.

"I used to write to Mum and Dad every Sunday and sometimes they would come and visit. There was no television so I would listen to the radio every night to hear the news from home.

"I stayed for four years and it was a very happy time. It has affected my life in such a good way. I still remember that feeling of being in such a lovely, safe village and I go back to visit every year."

CASE HISTORY
Rev Ron Smith, 61

Ron was evacuated from the East End of London when he was only 5.

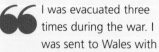

"I was evacuated three times during the war. I was sent to Wales with my brother when I was 9. It was not a happy experience.

"We went to a coal-mining village and I saw mountains for the first time in my life! Most people spoke Welsh, but we went to live with an elderly English couple who didn't treat us very well.

"I think they were forced to take us in because they had an extra

room. Not all the foster families wanted to look after an evacuee.

"All they fed us with was bread and margarine or potatoes and gravy. They even raided our food parcels! We were hungry all the time and often cold.

"We were treated virtually as slaves. We had to scrape out the dustbins and go looking for firewood.

"As an evacuee, you felt you didn't belong anywhere. Many evacuees have since had problems forming relationships. I think splitting up families is disastrous."

Reading and Writing

Read Maisie Seager's story (page 40). Then answer these questions by choosing the correct answer from the three answers given at the end of each sentence, and copying out the correct sentence. The first one has been done for you.

1 Maisie went to the country by (a) car (b) train (c) bus.

   Maisie went to the country by train.

2 Maisie travelled (a) with her parents (b) alone (c) with her sister.

3 The children went first to (a) the village school (b) the village church (c) the village hall.

4 Maisie and her sister lived with (a) a kind woman (b) an unkind woman (c) a strict woman.

5 The woman taught Maisie (a) to read (b) to play the piano (c) to knit.

6 Maisie's parents visited her (a) every week (b) sometimes (c) often.

7 Every night Maisie (a) watched TV (b) listened to the radio (c) went to the cinema.

8 Maisie lived with the woman for (a) two years (b) four years (c) six years.

9 Living with the woman was an experience Maisie (a) hated (b) enjoyed (c) disliked.

10 Maisie goes back to the village (a) every year (b) never (c) sometimes.

Reading, Speaking and Listening

In Pairs

● Read Ron Smith's story on page 40. In groups, answer these questions, then share your ideas in a class discussion.
   1 Where was Ron Smith sent?
   2 Who did he live with?
   3 How did they treat him?
   4 How did he feel while he was there?
   5 How was Ron Smith's experience different from Maisie Seager's?

● Discuss how you would feel if you were sent away from home. Talk about what you would miss most if you suddenly had to go and live in a strange family.

Imagine one of you is an evacuee and the other is a reporter. Role-play a scene in which the reporter interviews the evacuee. Before you begin, make a list together of questions for the reporter to ask the evacuee.

Sport at School

In this unit you will be learning about how to develop arguments. You will be discussing your views on various subjects, and learning how to write letters expressing your opinions.

SPEAK OUT:

Do you think there should be more sport at school?

Karen Li, 11

School's for learning

'We should be learning about History, Maths and English at school, not playing netball in the rain. So I think there's too much sport at school already!'

Abigail Richards, 11

Try something new

'I don't think there is enough sport at school. Sport is fun and keeps you fit. We could try new sports like squash, basketball and volley-ball.'

Martin Beal, 11

No time for games

'We have games for just one hour on Thursday afternoon, when we do athletics, football and netball. It's not nearly enough and by the time we've changed and sorted out the equipment, the lesson's nearly over.'

David Martinez, 12

Where's the fun?

'Sport should be fun. Why force us to run or play football if we don't want to? Those who like it can always play games after school.'

Speaking and Listening

- In groups, discuss these questions about sport at school.
  1 Do you think there should be more sports lessons?
  2 How often do you think there should be sports lessons?
  3 How long do you think sports lessons should be?
  4 Should there be more different sports for you to try?
  5 Should everyone have to take part, even if they don't like sports?

- Choose someone to report your ideas, and share your views in a class discussion.

Writing

Each write two or three sentences expressing your views on sport at school. Make a wall display of 'Our Views on Sport at School'.

Homework Matters

Here are some students talking about homework:

Homework is supposed to be good for you, but I don't think homework should be allowed. I work hard enough at school.

Leanne

I don't see why we have homework. Why should I have to spend my time doing schoolwork instead of watching TV and doing the things I want to do?

Christine

I think homework is important. We need to make sure we have learned what we have done at school.

Alex

Wazim

Homework helps you to do well in exams. The trouble is, there is so much of it. It takes me much longer to do than the teacher says it should.

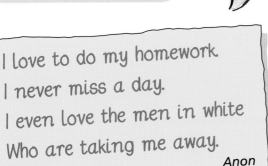

I love to do my homework.
I never miss a day.
I even love the men in white
Who are taking me away.

Anon

Speaking and Listening

In groups, discuss these views on homework.

- Whose view on homework do you agree with? Say why.
- Do you find it easy or difficult to get your homework done? Talk about any problems you have with homework.

Writing

Write a paragraph expressing your views on homework. Either use the title: 'Why I think homework matters' or: 'Why we shouldn't have to do homework'.

Letters to Newspapers

YOUR LETTERS

Time for Change

Why do shopkeepers put up signs saying 'Pocket-money items' when most of the items are over £2? Recently, I even saw one that was £6.

Children don't get this much pocket-money, so they just end up nagging their mums to get extra money. It's ridiculous!

Sarah Donaldson

Pets Aren't Prizes

I went to a fair recently and was shocked to see a man giving away goldfish in little plastic bags as prizes.

The tiny bags containing the fish were being swung around as if they were toys. My mum said this wasn't against the law, but I think this sort of behaviour is unacceptable.

Surely, cruelty such as this should be banned. What do other readers think?

Helen Cook

Waste High

It's terrible the way we waste so much water! A few weeks ago, a fire hydrant gushed in our road for nearly an hour. The water would have been much appreciated in developing countries.

Paul Baker

Skin Deep

I can't understand why people make such a big fuss about wearing fur, when wearing leather is just as bad. While fur is an animal's coat, leather is an animal's skin.

For many people wearing a fur coat is unthinkable. But many of the same people have leather shoes, belts and briefcases.

We should think more about whether an animal died for our luxuries.

Chandra Kapoor

NEW, IMPROVED!

Reading, Speaking and Listening

- In groups, read these letters. They were all written by children aged 11–14 to a newspaper for young people.
- Imagine that it is your job to award a £10 prize for this week's Star Letter, and a £5 prize to the runner-up. You should choose the two letters that state the reasons for their views most clearly, and that develop the most convincing arguments.
- When you have made your decision, choose someone to explain your choices to the rest of the class.

Writing

Which of the arguments in these letters do you agree with most strongly or disagree with most strongly? Write a reply to one of the letters, stating your views on the subject. Say why you agree or disagree with the writer's views.

Hard-Hitting Truth

The thing that annoys me most about adults is when they smack their children, and then tell the children off for smacking others. In some countries it is against the law to smack children and I think it should be here too.

My parents do not believe in smacking. In fact, they have never hit any of us and people often compliment them on our behaviour.

Children who are brought up with violence don't know any better. It leads to violence in the playground and then children suffer, when really it's their parents' fault.

Vijay Muckerjee

Talking Shop

I think it's a shame that little shops are forced to close because so many supermarkets are opening. This means that all the friendly shops, like the newsagents, chemists, bakers and butchers, are disappearing.

Supermarkets are putting a lot of people out of business. I think they should give smaller shops a chance. They're so much nicer to shop in.

Lisa Perry

Write to:
The Editor,
Teen News

Freedom Fight

I was very angry and upset when I read about all the recent violence and killings. We live in a rural area and my 5-year-old sister and I used to enjoy walks together, but now my parents don't like us going for walks, and will only let me go out by myself if I take one of our dogs.

People who murder are disgusting, particularly those who kill children. I was horrified by the Dunblane tragedy.

I don't think our freedom should be taken away by a few people. But if the situation continues, by the time my generation have children it will not be safe to let them out of sight.

Something must be done to let our children have the same freedom our parents had.

Emma Thorne

Writing a Letter to a Newspaper

When you write a letter to a newspaper, you should do it in stages, just as you did when writing your life story (see page 36). Here is how Sophie planned and wrote a letter about her views on Bonfire Night.

Stage 1:
Collecting ideas

Sophie found a piece of paper and did a brainstorm.

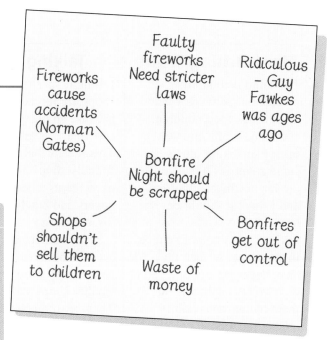

Faulty fireworks
Need stricter laws

Ridiculous – Guy Fawkes was ages ago

Fireworks cause accidents (Norman Gates)

Bonfire Night should be scrapped

Bonfires get out of control

Shops shouldn't sell them to children

Waste of money

Stage 2: Making a plan and writing the first draft

Sophie drew a flow chart. Making a flow chart helped her to plan the order in which she was going to put her ideas.

1 It's out of date
↓
2 Firework accidents
↓
3 Stop selling them to children
↓
4 Faulty fireworks: need stricter laws
↓
5 Bonfires get out of control
↓
6 Waste of money

Here is Sophie's first draft of her introduction.

I am writing to your newspaper to say why I think we should stop having Bonfire Night. I don't know why we go on celabrating something that happend hundreds of years ago. It's dangrous and it's a waste of money.

Stage 3: Revising and redrafting

Sophie showed her first draft to her teacher, before revising and redrafting it. He suggested that she should try to change the opening sentences, to make them grab the reader's attention and put across her view more strongly.

So Sophie changed them:

I think Bonfire Night should be scrapped. It's qite ridiculous to go on celabrating something that happend hundreds of years ago. It's dangrous and a waste of money.

Stage 4:
Checking the grammar, punctuation and spelling

Before copying out her letter to send it to the newspaper, Sophie checked her grammar, punctuation and spelling. She found four spelling mistakes in the first paragraph and corrected them:

She changed 'qite' to 'quite' 'celabrating' to 'celebrating', 'happend' to 'happened' and 'dangrous' to 'dangerous'.

Spelling Hint: Qu

In English, the letter **q** is always followed by the letter **u**. For example:
question   quarter
Copy out and complete these sentences by adding a word beginning with **q**.

1 An angry argument is called a ...

2 A woman married to a king is a ...

3 The noise a duck makes is ...

4 If there is no noise at all, it is ...

5 A line of people waiting for something is a ...

6 A competition which tests people's knowledge is called a ...

7 Another name for a pound is a ...

8 A sprinter runs very ...

Stage 5: Writing a neat copy

Sophie wrote out a neat copy of her letter and sent it to the newspaper.

tell the police and leave it at that.

Ranjit Bowman

Stop Bonfire Night

I think Bonfire Night should be scrapped. It's quite ridiculous to go on celebrating something that happened hundreds of years ago. It's dangerous and a waste of money.

Fireworks cause lots of accidents. Last year there was a boy from our estate called Norman Gates who got badly burned. He had a number of bangers in his pocket and they went off.

My friends think someone stupid dropped a match in his pocket. He had to have skin grafts and he'll be scarred for life.

People who sell fireworks to children should get heavy fines. I think fireworks should only be set off at public displays. But there can still be accidents because of faulty fireworks. I read about a vicar at a church fireworks party. He had bought some really big fireworks and when he lit them they exploded in his face. The fireworks came from abroad. There should be stricter laws

on firework safety.

Bonfires are dangerous, too. They can get out of control. The fire brigade get a lot of calls on Bonfire Night. This wouldn't happen if Bonfire Night was scrapped.

People waste lots and lots of money on fireworks, which only last a few minutes anyway. I think it's time we stopped celebrating Bonfire Night.

Sophie Pavner

Weather Report

Why do grown-ups talk so much about the weather?

Writing

- In pairs, discuss Sophie's letter. Which of her arguments do you agree with? Which of her arguments do you disagree with? What are your views on Bonfire Night?

- Write a letter together, in reply to Sophie's letter, giving your views on Bonfire Night. Draft your letter in stages, as Sophie did. Start by doing a brainstorm and making a plan, then draft and revise it, before checking it for mistakes and writing out a neat copy.

- On your own, write a letter to a newspaper on a topic about which you have strong views. Either choose your own topic or write about one of these topics:
    Cruelty to animals
    School uniform
    Teasing and bullying
    Looking after the environment
    Friendship and what makes a good friend.

Punctuation Practice – Apostrophes

The apostrophe is shaped like a comma. It looks like this ' and has two main uses.

One of its uses is to show where a letter or letters have been missed out of a word. The apostrophe is written in the word where the letter or letters are missed out. For example:

I didn't do it. (did not → didnot → didn't)

You're late. (you are → youare → you're)

She's not allowed out. (she is → sheis → she's)

We'll go together. (we will → wewill → we'll)

They've agreed to come.
   (they have → theyhave → they've)

Notice how two words, such as <u>did not</u>, become one word, <u>didn't</u>, when we use an apostrophe to shorten them. An unusual example is <u>will not</u>, which becomes <u>won't</u>.

Writing

Copy out these sentences, and use the apostrophe to shorten the words that are underlined. The first one has been done for you.

1 <u>I am</u> going out later.
   I'm going out later.
2 I <u>do not</u> know what to do.
3 He <u>has not</u> a clue where it is.
4 We <u>will not</u> be there long.
5 <u>It is</u> nearly time for the kick-off.
6 <u>They are</u> always late.
7 <u>We are</u> out of those, <u>I am</u> afraid.
8 <u>You are</u> right, I <u>should have</u> said no.

Checking for apostrophes

Sanjay wrote about animal cruelty in his letter to the newspaper. When he had revised and redrafted it, he asked Suzanne to check the punctuation for him. She noticed that he had not used apostrophes when he had shortened words and missed letters out.

Read through the first paragraph of Sanjay's letter, and make a list of all the words in which he forgot to put an apostrophe. Then write the list out again, this time with the correct punctuation.

I think its disgusting the way that people treat animals. Day by day, week by week, year by year, theres so much cruelty going on. Animals arent here just for us to do what we like with them. Theyve as much right to be on this planet as us.

In this unit you will be looking at some different types of poems, and writing some poems of your own. There are also some poems for you to read and perform.

Shape Poems

A **shape poem** is one in which the words or lines of the poem are arranged to make a picture or shape. A shape poem can be about any kind of object, such as a trumpet or a tree, a scarf or a sword, a bone or a boat. In the simplest form of shape poem, the words are written so that they make an outline picture of the object. There is an example on the right.

There are some more examples of shape poems below. In each poem the writer has arranged the words and lines so that they fit inside the shape of the object.

My apple

My big juicy apple, a scrumptious sight. It will soon be break time, then I'll take a bite.

Rosalyn Low

Snail

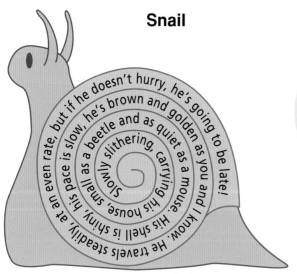

Slowly slithering, carrying his house, small, his pace is slow, he's brown and golden as you and I know. He travels steadily, at an even rate, but if he doesn't hurry, he's going to be late! His shell is shiny, quiet as a beetle and as a mouse.

Claire Pepperell

Balloon

as
big as
ball as round
as sun . . . I tug
and pull you when
you run and when
wind blows I
say polite-
ly
H
O
L
D
M
E
T
I
G
H
T
L
Y.

Colleen
Thibaudeau

The Scarecrow

I
AM
USED TO
BEING
A
SCARECROW, BUT SOMETIMES IN SUMMER
I WISH
I COULD
RUN ALONG
THE FIELDS
AND FEEL
THE FRESH
GRASS
UNDER
M
Y
S
T
R
A
W
FEET.

Ruth West

Reading, Speaking and Listening

In pairs, read the three poems ('Snail', 'Balloon' and 'The Scarecrow'), then answer these questions.

1 Which words and phrases in Claire's poem describe:
   (a) how small the snail is
   (b) how quietly it moves
   (c) its colour
   (d) how slowly it moves?

2 In her poem, Ruth imagines that the scarecrow is a person. What does she say the scarecrow wishes it could do?

3 (a) How does Colleen describe the size of the balloon?
   (b) How does she describe the shape of the balloon?
   (c) What does she imagine the balloon saying to the person who is holding it?

Writing

Write a shape poem in which you fit the lines of your poem inside the shape of an object or animal. Write your poem in stages:

1 Choose an object or animal with a shape that is easy to recognise. If you want, you can imagine that the object or animal can think and speak – in the way that Ruth and Colleen imagine that the scarecrow and the balloon can speak.

2 Make a list of words that you could use to describe the main features of the object.

3 Draft a short poem about the object describing one or two of its main features. (Note: a shape poem does not have to rhyme. It is more important to choose words that clearly describe the object's features than to make the poem rhyme.)

4 Draw an outline of the object in pencil.

5 Fit the words of your poem around the outline of the object.

6 Check the spelling and punctuation of the poem.

7 Make a neat copy of it. This could be either handwritten or done on a word processor.

List Poems

In the poems on the next three pages, the writers have developed their ideas in the form of a list.

Food I like

Burgers, sausages,
Chips and beans.
Jelly, ice-cream,
Tangerines.

Curry, chicken,
Chutney, cherries,
Apples, bananas,
Plums, strawberries.

Bacon, eggs,
Tomatoes, ham.
Cheese and crackers,
Cakes and jam.

Derek

Writing

Derek's poem (above) consists of a list of names of the food he likes. All the words in the poem apart from 'and' are nouns. Read about nouns (below) and then write your own list poem with the title either 'Food I Like' or 'Food I Hate'.

Nouns

A noun is the name of anything
like <u>car</u> or <u>soap</u> or <u>love</u> or <u>ring</u>.

A noun is the name of a person too
like <u>Jason</u>, <u>Wasim</u>, <u>Jill</u> or <u>Lou</u>.

A noun is also the name of a place –
<u>Pakistan</u>, <u>Glasgow</u>, <u>Mars</u> or <u>Space</u>.

A noun's any kind of naming word –
<u>bluebottle</u>, <u>Bill</u>, <u>Bolton</u>, <u>bird</u>.

Stuart Lewis

A **noun** is any word that is the name of a thing, a person, a feeling or an idea. In Stuart Lewis's poem, the nouns are underlined. Copy out the rhyme below and underline the nouns.

Little Jack Horner sat in the corner
Eating an enormous pie.
He stuck in his thumb
And pulled out a plum
And squirted the juice in his eye.

Anon

Mad meals

Grilled cork
matchbox on toast
glass soup
roasted clock
ping-pong balls and chips
acorn sandwich
fillet of calculator
trouser salad
grilled lamp-post
ice-cream (vanilla, soap
    or pepper)

Michael Rosen

Writing

- Read Michael Rosen's list of crazy foods in his poem 'Mad Meals' (above). Then write a similar poem of your own, with the same title.
- Write a mad menu for Crazy Clare's Café.
- Write a list poem about all the things you would put in a silly sandwich.

The next two list poems (on page 54) use verbs as well as nouns. Before you start reading the poems, read Stuart Lewis's poem about verbs and do the exercise that follows it.

Verbs

A verb is a special kind of word.

It tells you of something being done,

Like <u>swim</u> or <u>talk</u>, <u>eat</u> or <u>walk</u>,

<u>Creep</u> or <u>crawl</u> or <u>run</u>.

A verb is a word that tells you

what people and things are doing,

Like <u>shining</u> or <u>glowing</u>,

<u>Swallowing</u> or <u>chewing</u>.

Stuart Lewis

A **verb** is a word that tells us what people or things are doing or being.

In pairs

- Make a list of verbs that tell you about the things people do when they eat. Here is the start of such a list:
    eat, bite …
- Make a list of verbs that describe the different ways animals and people can move. Here is the start of such a list:
    walk, creep …

An A-Z of Animals

Here is the start of an alphabet poem about animals and what they are doing.

An alligator attacking

A bumblebee buzzing

A cat creeping

A dolphin diving …

Writing

In groups, your task is to complete the poem, following the same pattern. The verb that tells you what the animal is doing must begin with the same letter of the alphabet as the name of the animal. If you get stuck on any letter, use a dictionary to help you to find either the name of an animal or a suitable verb.

Note: X is very difficult, so use this line about a xiphias, which is a type of swordfish: 'A xiphias exploring'.

Have You Ever Heard … ?

Have you ever heard a conker crying?
Have you ever heard a wishbone sighing?

Have you ever heard a pencil splutter?
Have you ever heard a marble mutter?

Have you ever heard a wheelbarrow moaning?
Have you ever heard a mirror groaning?

Have you ever heard a saucepan roaring?
Have you ever heard a carpet snoring?

John Foster

Writing

In pairs or on your own, write some lines to add to John Foster's poem (left) about objects that behave in an unusual way. Here is an example of some lines that Louisa wrote:

Have you ever seen a motorbike crying?

Have you ever seen a lawn-mower flying?

Recipe Poems

A **recipe poem** is a poem that is set out like the instructions for a recipe in a cookery book. On the right is a recipe poem that Serena wrote.

Recipe for a Vampire

Take a spoonful of anger.
Stir in some strength and a pinch
of hate.
Sprinkle in the poisonous fangs
of a snake.
Cut the scales from a rat's tail.
Add the sharp teeth of a shark.
Mix together in a coffin.
Cover with bats' wings.
Boil until it bubbles.
Pour into an ice-cold mould.
Leave in a dark damp cave to set.
Then, in two days, you will have
a vampire.

Serena

Writing

Try writing your own recipe poem. A recipe poem can be about anything. On the right is a list of things you can write a recipe for.

Either choose something from the list or invent a subject of your own.

A MONSTER   A WIZARD
A TEACHER   A DRAGON
A HAUNTED HOUSE   AN ALIEN
A FAIR   A GHOST
A CLOWN   A DISCO

It may help you to follow these three steps:

1 Start by doing a brainstorm. Make a list of all the *ingredients* – the things you need to put in – to make whatever it is you are making.

2 Look at Serena's poem and notice how each of the sentences (except the last one) starts with a verb. That's because each of the sentences in a recipe is a command telling you to do something. So you will need to start each of the sentences in your recipe with a verb.

On the right is a list of some of the verbs you could use.

| pour | stir | mix | add | fry | cook | boil | simmer |
| peel | sprinkle | cut | slice | whisk | roast | grill | bake |

3 Now write your poem.

Limericks

The poems on this page are known as **limericks**. A limerick is a five-line verse, made famous by a writer called Edward Lear.

Reading, Speaking and Listening

- In pairs, take it in turns to read the poems aloud to each other.
- Each choose the limerick you think is funniest. Copy it out and learn it.

An adventurous lady called Florrie
Had a monster she kept in a quarry.
But it didn't like plants
And ate both of her aunts
Although later it said it was sorry.

Nick Timms

There was a young lady from Slough
Who went into school with her cow.
The cow was so bright
It got all its sums right
And it's two books ahead of her now.

Nick Timms

Our school has a bully called Ray
Who copies my homework each day.
So last night out of spite
I did none of it right.
Just my luck, 'cause today he's away.

Nick Timms

A heartless young fellow from Tweed
Took his dragon to school on a lead.
When he left it outside
It just sat there and cried
'Cause it wanted to learn how to read.
Nick Timms

There was a young fellow called Mark
Who would swim out to sea in the dark.
On these night-time trips
He saw lots of ships
Until he was seen by a shark!

Anon

There was a pop singer called Fred
Who sang through the top of his head.
It came as a blow
When the notes were too low
So he sang through his toe-nails instead.
Max Fatchen

Writing

Notice how each limerick follows a similar pattern, with two different rhymes and two different line lengths:

- lines 1, 2 and 5 are longer lines, and all end with the same rhyme;
- lines 3 and 4 are short lines, and end with the same rhyme.

Working in pairs or groups, complete this limerick:

There was a young fellow called Blair
Who couldn't get up from his chair.
He rang 999
(A short line rhyming with 'nine')
(A longer line rhyming with 'chair').

Now try to write a limerick of your own. Either make up your own first line or use one of these:

There once was a teacher called Pool …

A wizard's apprentice called Nell …

There once was a dentist called Jill …

A strict old headteacher called Blains …

A clever detective called Parr …

Make a class display of limericks. As well as the ones you have written, you could include copies of other limericks you find in books – from the poetry books in the classroom or in the poetry section in the library.

Poems to Read and Perform

In Pairs

- Practise reading and performing this poem, then either make a tape-recording of your reading or perform it to the rest of the class.

- Role-play a similar scene in which a teacher asks a pupil why their homework is late, and the pupil makes up excuses. Then, using the ideas that came up in your role-play, write your own poem called 'Excuses, Excuses'. Practise reading it together, then perform it to the rest of the class.

Excuses, Excuses

Late again Blenkinsopp?
What's the excuse this time?
  Not my fault sir.
Who's fault is it then?
  Grandma's sir.
Grandma's? What did she do?
  She died sir.
Died?
  She's seriously dead alright sir.
That makes four grandmothers this
  term Blenkinsopp
And all on PE days.
  I know. It's very upsetting sir.
How many grandmothers have you
  got Blenkinsopp?
  Grandmothers sir? None sir.
You said you had four.
  All dead sir.
And what about yesterday
  Blenkinsopp?
  What about yesterday sir?
You were absent yesterday.
  That was the dentist sir.
The dentist died?
  No sir. My teeth sir.
You missed the maths test
  Blenkinsopp!
  I'd been looking forward to it sir.
Right, line up for PE.
  Can't sir.
No such word as 'can't' Blenkinsopp.
  No kit sir.
Where is it?
  Home sir.
What's it doing at home?
  Not ironed sir.
Couldn't you iron it?
  Can't sir.
Why not?
  Bad hand sir.
Who usually does it?
  Grandma sir.
Why couldn't she do it?
  Dead sir.

                    Gareth Owen

In Groups

Prepare a performance of the poem on the right.

- Experiment with different ways of reading it. For example, talk about which lines you might read with only one voice and which lines you might say together.

- Try using some percussion instruments to help you to stress the poem's rhythm.

- Think about the actions and sound effects you could add.

- If you can use the stage or the drama studio, you might be able to add lighting effects.

Practise your performance, then present it to the rest of the class. When you have all finished, discuss whose performance worked the best and why.

Song of the Victorian Mine

Shut six men in a metal cage –
Wind them down, wind them down.
Drop them in a dismal pit –
Down in the mine,
Deep in the mine,
Dark in the mine all day.

Back the pony up to the cage –
Wind him down, wind him down.
Trip him up and make him sit –
Down in the mine,
Deep in the mine,
Dark in the mine all day.

Load the ore in the metal cage –
Wind it down, wind it down.
Waterlogged and candlelit –
Down in the mine,
Deep in the mine,
Dark in the mine all day.

Bring the canary in his cage –
Wind him down, wind him down.
He'll die first if the air's not fit –
Down in the mine,
Deep in the mine,
Dark in the mine all day.

Thirty thousand times in the cage –
Wind me down, wind me down.
Fill my lungs with grime and grit –
Down in the mine,
Deep in the mine,
Dark in the mine all day.

Sue Cowling

In this unit you will be reading and talking about myths and legends from different parts of the world.

Anancy and Mongoose

Reading and Writing

Here is a West Indian myth for you to read. Before you read the story, use the library to find out what a *mongoose* is and what an *opossum* is. As well as looking in reference books, look them up on a CD-ROM. Use the information you find to write three sentences about them, saying:

1 what they look like;

2 where they live;

3 what they eat.

Myths and legends are particular types of stories:

- A **myth** is a story that was made up long ago, often to explain the natural world and religious beliefs.

- A **legend** is an old story that was once believed to be true, but that is probably untrue.

Anancy and Mongoose – A story from Jamaica

All the creatures of the forest came to watch a <u>contest</u> between Anancy, the trickster spider, and the <u>sly</u> Mongoose. They wanted to see who was the most <u>cunning</u>, the most brave and the most <u>skilful</u>. The contest was to see who could catch the biggest snake.

'Yes, that's a really good test,' said Opossum.

'But everyone knows that Mongoose is the best snake-catcher in the forest,' said Fieldmouse. 'Anancy will never win.'

'Anancy is always <u>bragging</u> that he can do anything. Let's see!' laughed Squirrel.

'The winner will be the one who brings back the largest snake – alive!' yelled Monkey. 'They have two days to catch one.'

Anancy slunk away, looking sad. He did not know how he was going to catch a snake. Then he thought of a plan. He began to sing:

'Anancy is King!
Anancy is the best!
Anancy is the Master!
He will win the test!'

Two days later, the creatures gathered together in a <u>clearing</u> in the forest to see if Mongoose or Anancy would win.

'Anancy will lose this contest,' said Frog to Toad. 'He's met his match at last.'

Mongoose was the first to bring in a snake. It was bitten in two places, but it was still alive. All the creatures were <u>amazed</u> at its size. They clapped and cheered.

Meanwhile Anancy had met the longest snake in the forest.

'The other creatures do not believe you are the longest snake. If you let me carry you to them, I'll prove you are not only the longest snake in the forest, but the longest creature.'

The snake wanted to be known as the longest creature and <u>eagerly</u> agreed. Anancy asked the snake to wrap itself round a stick. Then he tied the snake to the stick.

'Just to make sure you don't fall when I carry you,' said Anancy.

All the creatures were amazed when Anancy brought the snake into the clearing. Once again Anancy had proved his skill. Mongoose was sad because he had lost and because his snake had died from its wounds. But everyone else joined in as Anancy sang:

'Anancy is King!
Anancy is the best!
Anancy is the Master!
Anancy won the test!'

Reading and Writing

- Put the following words in the order in which you would find them in a dictionary:
  contest sly cunning skilful bragging clearing amazed eagerly.
  Then use a dictionary to find out what each word means. Write the words out in alphabetical order, saying what each one means.

- Write sentences in answer to these questions:
  1 Why did the animals hold a contest?
  2 What did Anancy and Mongoose have to do to win the contest?
  3 Which creatures think that Mongoose will win?
  4 Why did the creatures clap and cheer when Mongoose came back to the clearing?
  5 Why did the snake agree to go to the clearing with Anancy?
  6 How did Anancy trick the snake?
  7 At the end of the story, why is Mongoose sad?
  8 How do you think Anancy felt at the end of the story?

Speaking and Listening

- Read the story aloud in groups, with one person taking the part of the storyteller and other people taking the parts of Anancy, Opossum, Fieldmouse, Squirrel, Monkey and Frog, and everyone joining in with the song at the end.

- Take it in turns to re-tell the story of Anancy and Mongoose to each other in your own words. Do not try to copy the version above, and don't worry if you miss some of the details out.

Tiddalik the Flood-maker

Reading

Here is a myth told in Australia by the aborigines. Some of the verbs have been left out; they are listed after the story. In groups, read the story and work out which word fits in which gap. Make a list of the words you choose, then compare your list with the lists other groups have made.

Note: The *wombat* is an Australian animal. The *kookaburra* and the *emu* are Australian birds.

Tiddalik the Flood-maker
An Australian myth

Tiddalik was a gigantic frog. One morning he ____1____ up feeling very, very thirsty. He started to drink. He went on and on ____2____ until there was no fresh water left in the world. Soon all the animals and plants were ____3____ because there was no water anywhere. It seemed that soon Tiddalik the frog would be the only animal left alive.

The other animals could not ____4____ what to do. Then a wise old wombat had an idea. Somehow they needed to make Tiddalik laugh. Then all the water that was ____5____ in his mouth would flow out.

All the animals went to where Tiddalik lived. One by one they ____6____ to make him laugh. The kookaburra ____7____ his funniest stories. The kangaroo ____8____ over the emu. The lizard ____9____ up and down on two legs with his belly sticking out. But Tiddalik just sat there. He didn't even smile.

The animals were desperate. Nothing seemed to amuse Tiddalik. Then the eel came along. He ____10____ to dance. He started slowly at first, then began to dance faster and faster. He ____11____ and turned. He ____12____ and squirmed. He bent himself into the oddest shapes. Tiddalik's eyes lit up. His mouth began to twitch and suddenly he burst out ____13____. And as he laughed, all the water came ____14____ out of his mouth and flowed away, filling up the lakes, the swamps and the rivers.

trapped   laughing   tried   dying   began
gushing   jumped   think   told   drinking
wriggled   waddled   twisted   woke

Reading and Writing

Write sentences in answer to these questions:

1 Why did Tiddalik drink up all the fresh water?

2 What started to happen because there was no water?

3 Why did the wombat suggest they should try to make Tiddalik laugh?

4 What things did the animals do that Tiddalik didn't find funny?

5 Suggest some other things the animals could have done to try to make Tiddalik laugh.

6 How did the eel make Tiddalik laugh?

7 What happened when Tiddalik laughed?

In Pairs

- Talk about how you could present the story of Tiddalik the Flood-maker as a picture-strip. Work out how many pictures you will need to have. Then, draw the pictures and write a caption for each one.

- Use the library to find out all you can about birds and animals that live in Australia, such as the kookaburra, the emu, the wombat, the kangaroo, the koala bear and the duck-billed platypus. Write three sentences about each one, saying:

  1 what it looks like;

  2 where it lives;

  3 what it eats.

Draw pictures and use your three sentences as captions. Use your pictures to make a wall display called 'Animals in Australia'.

Daedalus and Icarus

DAEDALUS AND ICARUS
A GREEK LEGEND

Daedalus was in trouble. He had argued with the King of Crete. The King wanted to kill Daedalus and his son Icarus. Somehow they must escape.

So Daedalus made some wings from birds' feathers. He made wings for Icarus, too. He planned to fix the wings to their bodies with wax.

When the wings were ready, he fixed on Icarus's wings. Then he put on his own. They were ready to fly across the sea to safety.

Before they set off, Daedalus spoke to his son. 'Your wings are stuck on with wax. Wax melts if it gets too hot. Do not fly near the sun or the wax will melt. Your wings will fall off and you will die.'

Icarus was excited. He wanted to fly like a bird. He was not really listening to what his father said.

Daedalus heard the sound of marching feet. It was the King's soldiers coming to kill them. Quickly, Daedalus and his son leapt off the balcony of their house. The soldiers rushed through the house

Reading and Writing

and saw them disappearing up into the sky.

Icarus laughed as he flew through the sky. He swooped down towards the sea like a bird. Then he flew upwards towards the sun. Higher and higher he flew until he was feeling very hot. He was too near the sun. The wax began to melt and the feathers started to drop off. Down, down he fell towards the sea. Faster and faster he fell, until he hit the sea and was killed.

Daedalus watched in horror as his son fell past him. If only Icarus had listened to his warning. But it was too late. Icarus was dead.

Here are ten statements about the story of Daedalus and Icarus. Some of them are true, some of them are false. Write down the numbers of the ones you think are *true* and the ones you think are *false*. Then compare your answers in a group discussion.

1 The King of Crete was a friend of Daedalus and Icarus.

2 Daedalus made wings from birds' feathers.

3 Daedalus stuck the wings on with glue.

4 Icarus listened carefully to what his father said.

5 Daedalus and Icarus left quickly because the soldiers were coming.

6 Daedalus and Icarus leapt off the balcony of the King's palace.

7 Icarus enjoyed being able to fly.

8 The sun made Icarus feel very hot.

9 Icarus fell into the sea because his wings caught fire.

10 The message of this story is 'If you don't listen to warnings, you may get badly hurt.'

Indian Stories

The Clever Servant

A merchant called his servants,
one, two, three,
'Who can fill this room
for one rupee?'

The first met a farmer
and bought a pile of straw.
He took it to the merchant
and spread it on the floor.

The second bought some earth
from an old ditch-digger
'Better!' said the merchant.
'This pile is bigger.'

But the third bought a candle
and lit it that night.
'The winner!' said the merchant.
'The room is full of light!'

Tony Mitton

Speaking and Listening

In pairs, discuss what happens in the story of the clever servant. Then prepare a reading of the poem to present to the rest of the class. Decide how you are going to share out the reading. You could each read two verses, or one of you could be the narrator and the other could be the merchant.

Writing

Re-tell the story of the clever merchant in your own words. Instead of writing four verses, write four paragraphs. You could start your first paragraph with these two sentences:

Once upon a time, there was a rich merchant. He wanted to find out which of his servants was the cleverest ...

Why Ganesh has an Elephant's Head

The goddess Parvati longed for a child. She was lonely because her husband, Lord Shiva, was often away for a long time.

One morning, after taking her daily bath, Parvati collected all the skin she had rubbed from her body. She moulded it into the shape of a baby boy. Then she breathed life into the figure. She was overjoyed when it began to move. Parvati called her son Ganesh.

Each day, Ganesh stood guarding the gate while his mother bathed. All went well until one day Lord Shiva arrived and demanded to be let in. Ganesh did not know him, so he refused to let him in. This made Lord Shiva so angry that he chopped Ganesh's head off.

When Parvati discovered what had happened, she was heart-broken.

'You've killed my child,' she sobbed. Lord Shiva knew he had to do something.

'Don't cry,' he said. 'I will put things right.' And he set off to find a new head for Ganesh. He decided that he would take the head from the first animal he found that faced north.

Soon he saw a huge elephant. It was the god Indra's elephant. But Lord Shiva had a promise to keep, so he cut off the elephant's head. He took it back to the palace and put it on Ganesh's body.

Parvati was delighted to have her child alive again. She loved his new shape and she thought he was a very special child. Indeed, Ganesh was so special that he became a friend and a god to the Hindu people.

Renuka Singh

Reading and Writing

Read the story of Ganesh, then work with a partner and discuss how you would re-tell the story as a picture-strip.

Decide how many pictures you would need, then draw the picture-strip and write captions for each of the pictures.

Beowulf and Grendel

Beowulf and Grendel: A British Legend

Scene 1 The hall of King Hygelac.
The King is seated on a carved wooden chair. Beowulf, one of his warriors, is standing beside him.

King It is my wish that you should go to Denmark. The King of the Danes needs your help. He has built a great hall so that his warriors can <u>feast</u> together and sleep safely at night.

Beowulf I have heard tell of it.

King The hall was built twelve years ago. But it has remained empty ever since the first night of feasting.

Beowulf Why is that?

King That first night a great feast was held. The Danes were laughing, singing and making music. Suddenly the door was flung open. Standing in the doorway was a terrifying figure – a wolf-man, a night-<u>stalker</u>. It was the creature they call Grendel.

Beowulf Grendel!

King Before he left that night, Grendel killed thirty warriors. He tore them <u>limb</u> from limb and crunched them in his great jaws.

Beowulf This is <u>grave</u> news. Thirty warriors in one night!

King Ever since, anyone who has dared <u>approach</u> the hall at night has died. Grendel's appetite is <u>immense</u>.

Beowulf I will do as you wish. I will go to Denmark with twelve of my bravest warriors and I will make sure that Grendel is killed.

Scene 2 The great hall of the King of Denmark.
Beowulf and his warriors are asleep on the floor beside the benches and tables. They are awoken by the noise of the door being flung open.

Grendel *(sniffing)* I smell meat, human meat. Tonight Grendel shall have a feast. *(He grabs a warrior.)*

Warrior *(screaming)* Help! Help! Put me down! Put me down!

Grendel Silence, fool! *(He bends his mouth towards the <u>warrior</u>, getting ready to bite.)*

Beowulf *(grabbing Grendel's arm and forcing it behind him in an arm-lock)* Enough! Let go of my friend! *(They struggle and Beowulf <u>wrenches</u> Grendel's arm off. Grendel gives a howl of agony and runs off into the night, leaving a trail of blood.)*

Beowulf *(holding up the arm)* Behold, I have beaten the monster. He will die through loss of blood.

Warrior What a <u>ghastly</u> sight! Look, his arm is grey and hairy. His hand is crooked like a claw.

(The Danish king arrives, having heard the noise of the struggle.)

Danish King You are strong and brave, Beowulf. Well done! You have freed us from this evil <u>fiend</u>. Tomorrow we shall have a feast.

Narrator But Grendel is not yet dead. In pain, and weak from loss of blood, he heads across the cliffs, making for his <u>lair</u>.

Dictionary Practice

- Put the following words in the order you would find them in a dictionary:

  feast stalker limb grave approach immense warrior wrenches behold ghastly fiend lair

- Then use a dictionary to find out what each word means. Write the words out in alphabetical order, saying what each one means.

Speaking and Listening

- In groups, prepare a reading of the script. First, make a list of all the people who speak, and work out how many people you will need to have in your group. Then give out the parts and practise your reading. Get the narrator to read all the stage directions.

- Discuss how you would perform these scenes, then act them out. Before you begin, talk about how you are going to stage the fight, in order to make it look realistic and to make sure that neither of the people playing Beowulf and Grendel gets hurt.

- If you were going to put on a performance of these scenes, you would need to decide what scenery and costumes to have. Each draw pictures showing: (a) what you think the Great Hall should look like; (b) the costumes you would have Beowulf and his warriors dressed in; and (c) what you would want Grendel to look like. Then share your ideas with other members of the group.

Writing

Imagine you were one of the warriors in the Great Hall who saw the fight between Beowulf and Grendel. How would you describe the scene to your comrades on your return to Britain? Write what you would say to them around the camp fire.

In this unit you will be learning about how to convey information. You will be practising taking messages and giving instructions. You will also be reading and writing information about schools and about a school trip.

Messages and Instructions

Reading

The following message was given in a school to form 7W by their form tutor at registration:

66 Instead of attending Mr Bowman's music class this afternoon, I want the whole class to go to the Library. Make sure you keep to the narrow concrete path, because the playground is being resurfaced. When you arrive at the Library, I want you to collect your notebooks from the Librarian, Mrs Smith. Then find a seat. You will be given a talk by Mr Gardiner from the Central Library about non-fiction books. If he finishes his talk early, you may borrow a book and read it quietly to yourselves. Got that? 99

Here are the notes that three pupils wrote down after listening to the message.

> Don't go to Mr Bowman's music lesson. Go to the library and don't walk on the playground. Get notebooks from Mrs Smith. Sit down and listen to talk. Borrow library book.

Salman

> 1. Don't go to music.
> 2. Go to library.
> 3. Sit down and listen to talk.
> 4. Choose a book.
> 5. Be quiet.

Lisa

> Not Bowman for music. but library. Stick to path. Collect notebook from Smithy. Get a seat. Gardiner's talk — non-fiction. Borrow book. Be quiet.

Dawn

Speaking and Listening

In pairs, discuss each set of notes.

● Are there any important pieces of information missing from: (a) Salman's notes; (b) Lisa's notes; (c) Dawn's notes?

● Decide whose notes you think are best. Then, compare your views in a class discussion.

Here is another message that was read out to a Year 7 group in assembly by their Head of Year, Mrs Griffin:

❝ We have had to change the arrangements for those of you going on tomorrow's trip. You are to meet the bus outside the entrance to Martins Lane instead of at the main entrance, and it will leave at 8.15 rather than 8.30. Your bus driver, Mr Shorthouse, will be taking you straight to the Waxworks and not to the Animal Sanctuary as planned. The Animal Sanctuary is closed tomorrow morning. You will arrive back at school at 2.30, and not 3.30 as we originally thought. You will be met on your return by Miss Pearce, who will take you to your form room. Those of you who have still got to give me your money, please see me straight after assembly. ❞

Writing, Speaking and Listening

In pairs:

- Decide which pieces of information are important in this message.
- Each write your own set of notes containing all the important information.
- Show them to your partner and check that you have included all the important points.

Giving Instructions

Get into pairs. One of you is on duty at the reception desk at the main entrance to your school. The other is a visitor. Take it in turns to explain to the visitor how to get to each of the following places in the school, starting from the main entrance: (a) the main hall; (b) the library; (c) the gym; (d) the music room; (e) your classroom.

Note: If you want to do so, you can either use a plan of the school or draw your own sketch map to help show them where to go.

School Rules

On the right is an extract from a list of school rules. It is taken from a handbook issued at a lower school to new students and their parents.

You must learn to take pride in your appearance

DISCIPLINE

Students are members of the school at all times, in or out of uniform. They are expected to behave in a manner that will bring credit to the school.

1. Buying and selling between students is forbidden at school.

2. The Laboratories, Gymnasium, Swimming pool and Craft rooms are out of bounds unless a teacher is present.

3. Students will have to pay for any damage they cause to school property, other than fair wear and tear.

4. Lower school students who lunch at school may not leave the school premises during the lunch hour without the permission of the Head or a member of the Senior Staff.

5. Smoking on the school premises is strictly forbidden.

6. Students must wear school uniform whenever they are on the school premises or on a school outing.

7. The following items are not to be brought into school: chewing gum, lighters, matches, cigarettes, fireworks, radios, personal stereos, CD players, knives, skateboards, roller blades.

8. Students who are late for school must report to the School Secretary.

9. Anyone with permission to leave school during lesson time must sign out in the signing out book in the school office.

10. Coats, scarves and hats must not be worn inside the school.

Speaking and Listening

In groups:

● Study the list of school rules and suggest possible reasons for each one.

● Which of the rules do you think is: (a) the most important; (b) the least important? List the rules in order of importance, starting with the most important and ending with the least important. Then compare your list with other people's lists.

● Students who break school rules may get punished. Go through this list of rules one by one and decide what punishment, if any, a student should get if she or he breaks a particular rule.

Writing

● The school rules given above do not tell you how students should behave in the classroom. In groups, draw up a detailed list of guidelines for classroom behaviour.

● Each use a word processor to make a copy of your list of guidelines. Call it 'The Classroom Code'.

Advice for New Students

Here is a sheet of advice for new students produced by Cary and Gerard.

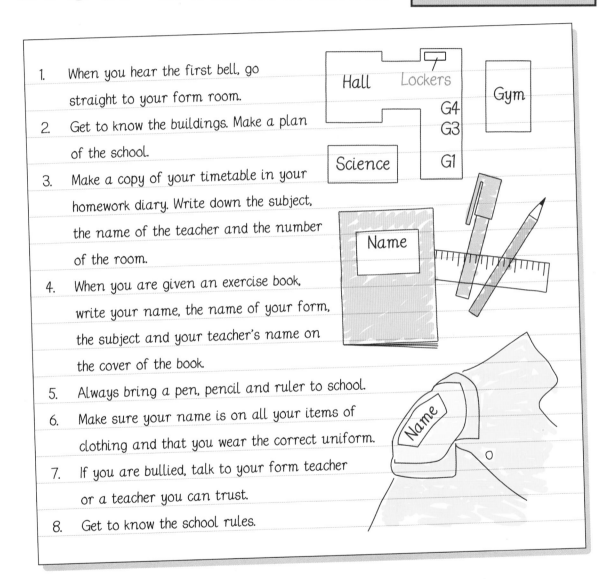

1. When you hear the first bell, go straight to your form room.
2. Get to know the buildings. Make a plan of the school.
3. Make a copy of your timetable in your homework diary. Write down the subject, the name of the teacher and the number of the room.
4. When you are given an exercise book, write your name, the name of your form, the subject and your teacher's name on the cover of the book.
5. Always bring a pen, pencil and ruler to school.
6. Make sure your name is on all your items of clothing and that you wear the correct uniform.
7. If you are bullied, talk to your form teacher or a teacher you can trust.
8. Get to know the school rules.

Speaking and Listening

In pairs, discuss what other advice you would give to new students joining your school. For example, what advice would you give concerning the following: *coats, bags, jewellery, valuables, bad weather, lost property, illness, stolen property?*

Writing

Use the word processor to draft, and then print out, your own sheet of advice for new students who are joining your school.

The Class Outing

Imagine that you are students in class 7R at Summerfield Comprehensive School, Lee Road, Redhampton. Your form tutor, Ms Robertson, wants you to organise your own end-of-term outing on Monday, 17 July. There are ten places nearby that you could go to, and you must choose which three to visit during the day.

Each place is only an hour's drive from the school, and they are all close to each other. So you only need to allow half-an-hour between visits to drive from one place to another.

You will leave school at 9.00 a.m., so you can start your first visit at 10.00 a.m. You must be back at school by 6.00 p.m. at the latest. At some point in your programme you must allow at least half-an-hour for lunch.

3 Morley Manor

The historic home of the Burton family. Visit the West Wing, which is said to be haunted by the ghost of Lucinda Burton. See Sir Marmaduke Burton's collection of vintage motor cycles. Enjoy yourself in the adventure playground in the park.

Open daily 10.00 a.m. to 5.00 p.m.

Time required: 2 hours

4 Royton Animal Rescue Centre

Wild and domestic animals from all over Britain are brought here for treatment. There are films and slide-shows of rescues taking place.
Open Monday–Friday 12.00 to 6.00 p.m.
Weekends 10.00 a.m. to 6.00 p.m.

Time required: 1 hour

1 Oldentown Stables

A tour of the stables, explaining how horses are trained for major races. You can see two famous horses, 'Flash' and 'Greased Lightning', who are trained at Oldentown.
Open Monday, Wednesday and Friday mornings only.

Time required: 1 hour

5 Saultown Butterfly Farm

Saultown has the largest indoor collection of butterflies in the world. Open daily 9.30 a.m. to 6.00 p.m.

Time required: 1 hour

2 WOODCHESTER ROMAN VILLA

Walk around the remains of a Roman fort and villa. Visit the museum and then follow the nature trail, a mile-long walk into open countryside.
Open Tuesday–Sunday 9.00 a.m. to 6.00 p.m. Closed on Mondays.

Time required: 2 hours

6 Lawson Park Zoo

See birds and animals from all over the world. Lawson has the country's largest collection of wild cats.

Open daily 9.00 a.m. to 6.00 p.m.

Time required: 1 hour

7 Camfield Swimming Pool

A chance to swim in one of the area's most popular swimming pools.

Open to the public
12.00–9.00 p.m.
Weekends
10.00 a.m.–
9.00 p.m.

Time required: 1 hour

8 Great Angle Abbey and Mill

*S*ee the abbey ruins and search for its famous ghosts. The gardens are ideal for a picnic lunch. The water mill is still working, and visitors can see a demonstration every afternoon.

The Abbey and grounds are open 9.00 a.m. to 6.00 p.m. (The water mill demonstration is at 2.30 p.m.)

Time required: 1 hour

9 CAMFIELD WAXWORKS

The largest waxworks outside London. See the Prime Minister and your favourite football player together in wax. Visit the dungeon and learn how prisoners were treated in the Dark Ages.

Open daily, 9.00 a.m. to 4.00 p.m.

Time required: 1 hour

10 Bexford War Museum

Find out what life was like during the **Second World War** – learn about mines and air-raid shelters, gas masks and food rationing. There is a large **tank collection**

and a film about **London during the Blitz**.
Open daily 10.00 a.m. to 6.00 p.m.

Time required: 2 hours

Speaking and Listening

In groups, decide which three places you would like to visit, then work out a travel programme.

Your teacher may have a copy of the Travel Programme sheet from the Teaching Resources Book, or you could make your own Travel Programme sheet by dividing a piece of paper into two columns. Put the heading 'Time' in one column and 'Programme' in the other column. Here is the start of the Travel Programme that Leanne, Halema and Tristan planned:

Time	Programme
9.00 a.m.	Depart school
10.00 a.m.	Arrive Oldentown Stables
11.00 a.m.	Depart Oldentown Stables
11.30 a.m.	Arrive Lawson Park Zoo

Letters

Reading and Writing

Read the letter about the end-of-term trip and then write sentences in answer to these questions.

1 Which students are going on the trip?

2 When is the trip?

3 Which two places are the students going to visit?

4 At what time must the students be at school?

5 Why do the students have to get to school early?

6 What advice about clothes does the letter give?

7 What does the letter say about lunch?

8 What else are the students asked to bring?

9 At what time will the students get back to school?

10 What does the letter say about the buses to the villages?

Whiteoaks Secondary School
Endersby Way
Camfield
Camfieldshire
CZ13 OAK

28 June 2001

Dear Parents/Guardians

As you know, we have organised an end-of-term trip for Year 7 students to visit Sowerby Pig Farm and the Rare Breeds Centre on Monday 12 July 2001.

All students are to arrive in school at 8.30 a.m. to register early. The special tour bus will leave school at 8.40 a.m., so it is important for everyone to arrive on time.

Students will need to bring a packed lunch and to wear outdoor, weather-proof clothing – it does rain sometimes, even in July! Wellington boots are advisable, as the pig farm gets muddy and dirty.

There will be a special guide, who will give a talk at the Rare Breeds Centre. Students are asked to bring their own pens, but notepads will be provided by the school.

We expect the tour bus to return to the school by 3.00 p.m., in time for parents to collect students, if they wish to do so. The school buses will not depart for the villages until the tour bus arrives back at school.

Yours faithfully

Pamela A. Studley
Head of Lower School

Writing

Imagine that your form tutor, Ms Robertson, has agreed to take you on the trip to the three places that you chose from the ten places described on pages 74–75. Now that you have chosen where to go, she has asked you to use the word processor to draft a letter for her to send out to parents.

Before you start drafting the letter, make a list of all the information you will need to put in the letter. On the right is the list that Hasan made.

- Date of trip.
- Places we're visiting.
- Time we must be in school.
- Time bus leaves.
- Lunch details.
- Advice on clothes.
- Items we need to take.
- Time bus gets back to school.
- Arrangements for getting home.

Laying Out a Letter

Make sure you lay your letter out properly.

- Be sure to put your address in the top right-hand corner.
- Put the date on which you are writing the letter.
- Start the letter properly with 'Dear Parents/Guardians'.
- Remember to use paragraphs, and to leave a line space between paragraphs.
- End the letter with 'Yours faithfully'.
- Sign your name clearly.

On the right is the start of Hasan's letter.

Summerfield Comprehensive School
Lee Road
Redhampton
RF2 1PZ
23 June 2001

Dear Parents/Guardians

I have arranged an end-of-term trip for the members of Form 7R on Monday 12 July 2001. The class voted on where they would like to go and we shall be visiting the following places –

ADVICE AND WARNINGS

In this unit you will be looking at ways of giving advice and warnings. You will be studying advice about water safety and cycling safety, and about what to do in an emergency. You will also be reading a cautionary tale, and then making up your own cautionary tale.

Swimming Pools Are Safer

The picture-strip on page 79 gives some advice explaining why it is safer to swim in your local swimming pool rather than outdoors, in places such as rivers and lakes.

Speaking and Listening

- In pairs, discuss the advice given in the picture-strip. Divide a piece of paper into two columns. In the first column, list all the reasons why it is dangerous to go swimming in outdoor places, such as rivers, lakes and canals. In the second column, list the reasons why swimming pools are safer.

- Then, role-play a scene in which two young people have an argument. One of them wants to go swimming outdoors in a lake, river or canal. The other person doesn't think it's safe, and wants to go to the local swimming pool instead.

Writing and Drawing

Design a poster to warn children of the dangers of swimming in outdoor waters, such as rivers, lakes and canals.

Swimming Pools are Safer

1   Swimming pools are safer

It's dangerous to swim outdoors in rivers, canals and lakes or in ponds, reservoirs and disused quarries. Over 80% of drownings happen in such places.

2   Swimming pools are warmer

The water in lakes, ponds, reservoirs and quarry pits can be very cold. The coldness of water is often a major cause when someone drowns.

3   The depth is marked

This means you can avoid getting out of your depth, and you know where it's safe to jump in.

4   The water is clean and clear

In rivers, lakes and canals you often can't see the bottom. You may cut yourself on something sharp or get trapped in weeds, branches or other obstacles.

5   There are no currents

There is no risk of being swept away by a current in a swimming pool.

6   You can climb out easily

There are steps if you want to get out. The banks of a river may be crumbly or slippery or a canal might have high walls.

7   There are trained lifeguards

When you go swimming in a river or lake there is no one to help you if you get into trouble. At a swimming pool there is always a trained lifeguard on duty.

8   There is rescue equipment available

The rescue equipment at swimming pools is checked regularly. At lakes, rivers and canals there may be no equipment available or it may have been damaged by vandals.

Be Safe in the Saddle

Be Safe in the Saddle

Eric Johnson offers some tips to help you cycle safely

Cyclists are more at risk of having a road accident than any other road users except motorcyclists. Young people are more likely to have a cycling accident between the ages of 12 to 14 than at any other age, and boys are five times more likely to get hurt than girls. You are most at risk on a bicycle when you are either turning right, going round a roundabout or crossing the pavement.

Turning right

When you're turning right, look behind you to check for traffic. If it's clear, give an arm signal early. Then move towards the centre of the road to take up the correct position for turning. Repeat the arm signal and give a last 'life-saver' look over your right shoulder before turning.

At roundabouts

You have to give way to traffic coming from the right. It is usually safer to stay in the left-hand lane all the way round. But you need to watch out for vehicles wanting to cross your path to leave the roundabout.

Crossing the pavement

Lots of accidents are caused by children riding across the pavement and straight out into the road. You should wheel your bicycle across the pavement and then wait for a gap in the traffic.

At night

Riding at night is dangerous because it can be difficult for drivers to see you. It is against the law to ride without lights and a reflector. It is also a good idea to wear something bright which reflects in a car's headlights. Another thing you can do is to fix reflectors on the pedals.

Safety equipment

Some of the most serious injuries are caused when people fall off and hit their heads. There is no law saying you must wear a helmet when 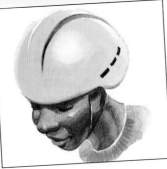 you cycle, but many people choose to do so. If you wear a helmet, make sure that it fits you properly and that it doesn't prevent you from seeing and hearing clearly.

The Highway Code

When you ride on the road, you must obey the traffic signs and signals. It is against the law to ride recklessly, so you mustn't play games or do stunts on the road. You should always ride in single file on busy narrow roads.

Carrying things

It is an offence for you to give someone else a ride on your bicycle, because it could easily cause an accident. If you want to carry things, it is  best to strap them onto the top of a rack behind the saddle. Slinging a bag over the handlebars can be dangerous, because it might slip and get caught in the spokes. If you ride with a bag over your shoulder, it can cause you to lose your balance.

Looking after your bicycle

Like any piece of equipment, your bicycle needs to be checked regularly. You need to keep the chain well oiled. Each week you should check that the brakes are working properly and that the tyres are hard enough and are not worn or damaged.

Reading

Read the article 'Be Safe in the Saddle' on page 80. Here are ten statements based on the information and advice given in the article. Some of the statements are *true* and some of them are *false*. Work in pairs, and decide which statements are true and which are false.

1 Cyclists are more at risk than any other road users.

2 Between the ages of 12 and 14, boys are five times more likely to get hurt in cycling accidents than girls.

3 Lots of accidents happen when cyclists are turning right.

4 It is usually safer to stay in the left-hand lane at roundabouts.

5 You are not allowed to ride a bicycle at night unless you wear bright clothing.

6 You must always wear a helmet when you ride a bicycle.

7 When riding on the road, cyclists have to obey all traffic signs and signals.

8 You are allowed to carry a passenger on your bicycle if you want to do so.

9 The best way to carry things on your bicycle is over your shoulder.

10 It is important to check your brakes and tyres once a week.

Speaking, Listening and Writing

In pairs, look through the advice given in 'Be Safe in the Saddle'. Then divide a piece of paper into two columns and make lists of 'Do's' and 'Don'ts' for cyclists.

Writing

Choose the ten most important pieces of advice given in the article. Then use the word processor to draft and design a sheet of advice for junior school children. Call it 'Ten Tips for Safer Cycling'.

How to Phone for Help

Speaking and Listening

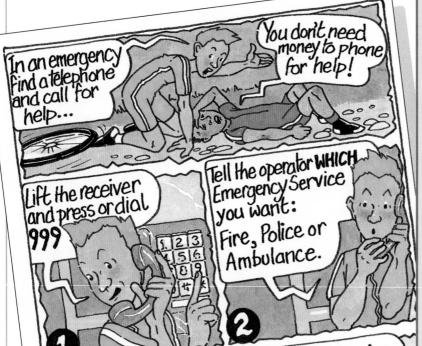

- Study the information about how to make an emergency telephone call.
- Imagine that you are walking down Forest Road, Newton. You see a boy fall off his bicycle and hit his head on the road. There is a telephone box on the corner of Forest Road, near The Fox and Hounds pub. The number of the telephone in the box is Newton 543953.
- In groups of three, role-play the conversation in which you call an ambulance. Do it three times, taking it in turns to be the person reporting the accident, the operator and the ambulance officer.

Spelling – Making Plurals

The word **plural** means 'more than one'.

The plural of a word is used to tell us that there is more than one of something.

For example, the word *chairs* tell us that there is more than one chair.

The foxes hid in the boxes

Making Plurals

There are two common ways of making plurals.

1 By adding an <u>s</u> to the word.

This is the most common way to make a word plural. For example:
cup → cup<u>s</u>   hand → hand<u>s</u>
bottle → bottle<u>s</u>

2 By adding <u>es</u> to the word.

- Words that end in <u>-x</u> add <u>es</u>. For example:
  fox<u>es</u>, box<u>es</u>

- Words that end in <u>-sh</u> add <u>es</u>. For example:
  brush<u>es</u>, dish<u>es</u>

- Words that end in <u>-ch</u> add <u>es</u>. For example:
  lunch<u>es</u>, peach<u>es</u>

- Words that end in <u>-ss</u> add <u>es</u>. For example:
  dress<u>es</u>, glass<u>es</u>

Spelling Practice

Copy out these sentences. Change the words in the brackets to their plurals by adding either <u>s</u> or <u>es</u>.

1 We washed up all the (plate) and (dish).

2 The pack of (hound) chased the (fox).

3 We bought three (apple) and three (peach).

4 There were (flower) on all the (bush).

5 We dipped the (paintbrush) in the (tin) of paint.

6 His (leg) were covered in (scratch).

7 We sat on the (bench) and ate our (sandwich).

8 We packed the (dress) in the (box).

9 Each of the (princess) had three (wish).

10 I wrote the (address) on the (envelope).

Cautionary Tales

A **cautionary tale** is a story that warns the reader not to do something. It explains what will happen to them if they ignore the warning.

Here is a poem about a boy who was always boasting.

The Boy Who Boasted

John Bragger was born with a very big head:
it grew bigger and bigger with all that he said.

He boasted, 'I'm braver and better than you.'
He boasted so much that his face became blue,

and he almost arrived at a premature death
from boasting so much that he ran out of breath.

'I'm the fastest,' he boasted, 'at running in school,'
but everyone knew that he wasn't at all.

'I'm the quickest at sums,' he continued, 'I'm bright.'
(He was quickest, but none of his answers were right.)

'I'm loudest at singing.' (We won't deny that,
but he sang even worse than the caretaker's cat.)

At most things in school, in fact, John was the worst,
but his head grew so big that we thought it would burst.

He could only just manage to squeeze through the door:
we were sure that it couldn't increase any more,

but it did and we even began to feel sorry
when he had to be taken to school in a lorry.

He carried on boasting about his success:
'I'm the best playing football. I'm brilliant at chess.

'I'm dead good at music. I've made an LP.
They've said I can have my own show on TV.

'I'm so rich that I'll soon be a millionaire.'
At times passers-by used to stop off and stare,

for he couldn't fit now into classrooms at all
and a crane had to lower him into the hall.

His brain was no bigger, I'd say, than a prune
but his head was the size of a hot-air balloon.

We thought it might happen, and it did so one day –
he boasted so much that he floated away.

He got smaller and smaller and higher and higher,
still boasting away (what a terrible liar):

'My computer's the biggest that anyone's seen.
Did I tell you last week I had tea with the Queen?

'Once I rowed in a boat down Niagara Falls.
My dad is a film star. My mum's won the pools.

'The American president told me next June
I can go in a rocket and visit the moon.'

With hardly a pause he continued to boast
as he soared over London and then to the coast,

but where he is now it seems nobody knows –
I suppose it depends on the way the wind blows.

(So maybe one day if you look up you'll spy
a huge head with legs drifting high in the sky.)

Our teacher pronounced, 'It's a bit of a mess,'
and various stories appeared in the press.

Then the council came round and collected their crane
and the school returned, almost, to normal again.

For now that he's gone I can honestly say
that we miss him a lot in an odd sort of way.

Charles Thomson

Speaking and Listening

- In groups, suggest some other boasts that John Bragger might have made before he blew away.
- Role-play the news report that appeared on local TV on the day that John Bragger floated away. You could include a number of interviews, for example, with his parents, his teacher and some of his classmates. Show the different attitudes people have to his disappearance, and end with an interview with a TV weather presenter who tries to forecast where the wind will blow him.
- Prepare a reading of the poem to present to the rest of the class. You will need a group of at least three people – one to tell the story, one to be John Bragger and one to be the teacher. If there are more than three of you, then you could experiment with having more than one storyteller.
- Practise your reading, then either tape-record it or perform it to the rest of the class. Afterwards, discuss whose reading worked best and why.

Writing

Make up a cautionary tale of your own. You could present it in the form of either a poem, a story or a comic-strip. Either develop an idea of your own or use one of these ideas:

- Raymond Gee who was addicted to TV;
- Pamela Groom who never tidied up her room;
- Belinda Beith who never ever cleaned her teeth.

In this unit you will be reading and writing scripts. You will be looking at how to write the script for a radio play, for a music programme and for a comedy programme.

Playscripts

Nasim's First Day

Scene: A classroom in a comprehensive school.
There is a knock on the door. Nasim enters. She is clutching a Marks and Spencer's carrier bag full of school books. Her hair is in long plaits. She is wearing a new school uniform that is too big for her, with baggy trousers underneath her school skirt.

Mr Bead: Come in. Come and meet the class.

(Nasim walks across and stands shyly facing the class.)

Mr Bead: Would you like to tell me your full name?

Susan: *(in a loud whisper)* Baggy pants!

(The girls on the back row next to Susan start giggling.)

Mr Bead: *(loudly and angrily)* That's enough, you lot. Now then, what's your Christian name?

Nasim: *(quietly)* I'm not Christian, Sir. Muslim. Sorry.

Mr Bead: *(smiling)* Of course. What are you called?

Nasim: Nasim, Sir.

Mr Bead: *(pointing to a desk in front of the teacher's table)* Sit there, Nasim. No one ever sits there. I can't think why. The rest of you talk quietly till the bell goes. I'll have a chat with Nasim.
(to Nasim) Right, I'm Mr Bead. I'm your form teacher, and I take you for Geography as well. I don't teach you today.

Nasim: No, Mr Bead.

Mr Bead: Where did you learn English, Nasim?

Nasim: In a place near Mirpur.

Mr Bead: Is that in Pakistan or India?

Nasim: Pakistan, Mr Bead.

Mr Bead: And how long have you been in England?

Nasim: One week.

Mr Bead: Are all your family here?

Nasim: No, Mr Bead.

Mr Bead: Who are you living with?

Nasim: My Uncle Assan and Aunt Zarniga. And my brother is here and my uncle's children.

Mr Bead: Your cousins.

Nasim: Yes, my cousins.

Mr Bead: I hope you will be happy with us, Nasim.

Nasim: Yes, Mr Bead.

(The bell rings. Nasim reaches down for her bag.)

Mr Bead: No, you stay here. I have to go and teach another class. What's first lesson, Martin?

Martin: English, Sir.

Mr Bead: Good. Miss Peters will be in soon. She's very nice.

Nasim: Yes, Mr Bead.

Speaking and Listening

- In groups, read the script aloud two or three times, taking it in turns to be Nasim. It is Nasim's first day, so when you are reading her part try to show how shy and nervous she feels.
- Role-play a scene at break, in which some of the other children gather round Nasim and ask her questions about herself, her family and her life in Pakistan. Do the scene twice. First, act out a scene in which the other children are friendly. Then, act out a scene in which the other children make fun of her and bully her.

In Pairs

- Imagine that later in the day Mr Bead finds Nasim on her own, looking upset. Role-play the scene in which Mr Bead asks her what's wrong.
- Talk about all the things that might have happened to Nasim on her first day. Then role-play a scene in which her uncle or aunt asks her about her day.

Writing

Write a script based on one of your role-plays. Follow the instructions below to make sure you lay out your script properly.

- Start with details of where the scene is taking place. For example:
  Scene: The playground at Nasim's school.
- Put the name of the person speaking in the margin.
- Every time a new person speaks, start a new line.
- Do not use speech marks.
- Put any instructions about how to speak inside brackets. For example:
  Mr Bead: (angrily) How dare you do that!
- Put any stage directions in brackets. For example:
  (Nasim walks towards the gate.)

Radio Scripts

When you listen to a play on the radio, you cannot see what the characters are doing. You have to be able to understand what they are doing from what they say. Sound effects are also used to help you to understand what is going on.

Here is part of a radio script. (FX means sound effects.)

The Things From Out There

FX: *Unearthly music as if made by a computer.*

Presenter: The Things From Out There – Episode 4.

FX: *A whining noise followed by a loud explosion.*

Juan: Another one crashed, Anna.

Anna: *(nervously)* Where are they coming from? What do you think, Juan?

Juan: I wish I knew. I *know* what the doctor said when she examined the body!

Anna: You never told me … you never told me what she said.

Juan: She said the body wasn't human.

Anna: But it *has* to be.

Juan: *You* didn't see the body. *(pause)* It was small and round. And the eyes. They peered at you, as if they could see right through you.

FX: *A clatter as if a dustbin has been knocked over.*
The sound of running footsteps.

Anna: What was that?

Juan: Someone's coming.

FX: *A door crashes open.*

Carol: *(hysterically)* Quick. There's been an accident. Something fell on Michael. He's over by the barn.

FX: *Loud unearthly music which gradually fades.*
The sound of someone groaning.

Juan: Michael! Michael! Are you all right?

Speaking and Listening

- In groups, prepare a reading of this script, together with sound effects. (Read the advice below on how to produce sound effects.)

- When you are ready, perform your reading for the rest of the class, or make a tape-recording of it.

Writing, Speaking and Listening

- In groups, discuss what might happen in the rest of the episode. Talk about what other characters might come into it, and whether or not the Things From Out There will speak.

- Each write a script for the rest of this episode. When you are ready, compare your scripts. Pick out the best parts from the different scripts and work together to produce a joint script. Then prepare a reading of your joint script, together with sound effects, and present it to the rest of the class.

Making Sound Effects

The sound effects you hear on the radio are often not tape-recordings of those actual sounds. They are made in various different ways. Here are some examples of the ways that some sounds can be made:

- The sound of a fire can be made by crunching up an old crisp packet or pieces of tinfoil.

- The sounds of animals and birds can be made by humans. For example, the hoot of an owl, the howl of a wolf.

- Spooky sounds can be made by scratching glass or by the squeaking hinges of a door.

Speaking and Listening

- In pairs, suggest ways that you might make sound effects for some of the sounds in the list on the right.

- Experiment with different ways of making some of these sounds. Then take it in turns to tell the rest of the class how you tried to make the sounds. You could tape-record the sounds and play them back to show which ones worked best.

a gunshot   a thunderstorm

feet on a gravel path

a car braking suddenly

an ambulance siren   a church bell ringing

a floorboard creaking

Radio Programmes

Writing, Speaking and Listening

You are a disc jockey for a new local radio station called Radio Jasmin. Choose some CDs to play on your show, and write a script to introduce your show and to link the different musical items. Then get a partner to help you to tape-record your show.

On the right is an example of such a script.

Kev: Here we are again at Radio Jasmin, also known as Radio 667. I'm Kev Murphy, and I just want to take this opportunity to say good morning to you all.

(Silence)

I SAID good morning.

(Silence)

No reply? *(laughs)* I'll wait. Now, put down your orange juice, your cereal spoons *and that piece of toast* and all say together – Good morning, Kev.

(Silence)

That's better ... now, here's something that'll get you wide awake and ready to go, this bright and beautiful morning. It's one of your favourite songs in the local charts at the moment.

(Music starts to play)

'Stone Love' by The Washer Band.

(The CD plays)

Did you enjoy that? I'll bet you did. Well, you don't want to miss out, then, do you? I want to see you all at 'The Queen's Head' in Fisher Road tonight, starting 7.30 p.m. The Washer Band will be there and so will I. So don't forget to tell your friends. Talking of friends, guess who's here to bring you bang up-to-date with what else is happening today. Good morning, Michaela.

Michaela: Good morning, Kevin.

Kev: But before she does, here's another piece of music by someone who I'm sure we're going to be hearing lots, lots more of. Genevieve Jenkins with her latest hit 'I Don't Know What I'd Do'.

(Music starts to play)

In Groups

Imagine that your school has started a lunch-time radio station, which broadcasts once a week on Mondays. The broadcast includes a five-minute item of news and information about forthcoming events.

- Plan and script this week's item, giving up-to-date news and information about events in your school.

- Then tape-record your 'School News' and take it in turns to play your recordings to the rest of the class.

Below is a short example.

Gita: Here we are at Radio Delgrado ... and I'm Gita Hussain, broadcasting from the Delgrado Community School. We have the following items on the agenda this lunchtime ...

FX: *Sound of crushed crisp packet.*

Gita: Yes ... I'm munching my lunch because the first item for discussion is ... are school lunches worth eating? With me is Miss Sandi Arfax from Year 8. She thinks lunches are good to eat.

FX: *Cheering.*

Gita: And arriving in the studio right now is Mr Philip Granger from Year 9. He can't stand another forkful. Just before Sandi speaks to us ... we have two interesting events. The Delgrado rave for Years 7, 8 and 9 takes place tonight in the lower school hall. Ticket only ... buy them from the lower school office now! And our favourite teacher ...

FX: *Clapping.*

Gita: Ms Elliot is spending the whole of the Easter holidays walking for charity. Exclusive interview later ... now back to Sandi.
Why do you think school lunches are worth eating, Sandi?

Comedy Programmes

Here is the script of a comedy show starring two comics.

I say, I say, I say

1st comic: I say, I say, I say. A funny thing happened to me on the way to the theatre.

2nd comic: Oh yes, what was that?

1st comic: I was riding in a bus.

2nd comic: So what happened?

1st comic: The conductor turned me off. They don't allow horses on buses.
(Laughter)

1st comic: Talking of jewellers.

2nd comic: Were we talking about jewellers?

1st comic: No, but we are now. Talking of jewellers. What's the difference between a jeweller and a jailor.

2nd comic: I don't know, what's the difference between a jeweller and a jailor?

1st comic: One sells watches, and the other watches cells.
(Laughter)

2nd comic: That reminds me. My budgie died.

1st comic: Your budgie died! How?

2nd comic: I washed it in Omo.

1st comic: I told you Omo wasn't good for budgies.

2nd comic: It wasn't the Omo that killed it, it was the spin dryer.
(Laughter)

1st comic: Do you know, every day my dog and I go for a tramp in the woods.

2nd comic: Does the dog enjoy it?

1st comic: Yes, but the tramp's getting a bit fed up.
(Laughter)

2nd comic: Did you know they're crossing sheep with kangaroos?

1st comic: Whatever for?

2nd comic: To make woolly jumpers.
(Laughter)

Writing

- In pairs, write your own script for a comedy show starring two comedians. As well as using jokes that you have been told by friends, include jokes that you have heard on radio and television. Look at joke books and copy out any good jokes that you find. (All the jokes in the script on the left were taken from a book of jokes.)

- When you have finished, practise your script, then perform it to the rest of the class.

Accents

Everyone speaks with an **accent**. Your accent is the way you pronounce words. Your accent is usually influenced by where you live when you are growing up, and by the people you live with. That's because when we are speaking, we tend to copy the people we hear.

So, people from different countries speak English with different accents. Also, people from different parts of Britain often speak with different accents.

In Pairs

- Use a tape-recorder to collect examples of people speaking with different accents. People you could record are: students and teachers at your school; your relatives; friends and their families.

- Ask the people you record to tell you a little bit about themselves. For example, get them to say when they were born, where they lived up to the age of 11 and which schools they went to. Ask them to describe what sort of an accent they think they have.

- Then listen to your recordings in class, and discuss what you have found out about people's accents.

Speaking and Listening

How many different accents can you think of?

- In groups, make a list of people you hear on the radio and see on TV who have different accents. Here is the start of such a list:

Name of person or programme	Accent
Neighbours	Australian
Brookside	Liverpool

- One of the features of your accent is the way you pronounce the vowels (the letters **a e i o u**) in the words you speak. Take it in turns to try saying this sentence in some of the different accents you have listed:

  After work my grandfather had a bath in a tub of hot water.

- People sometimes say that a person has a 'posh' accent. What do they mean? Discuss what you think a posh accent is.

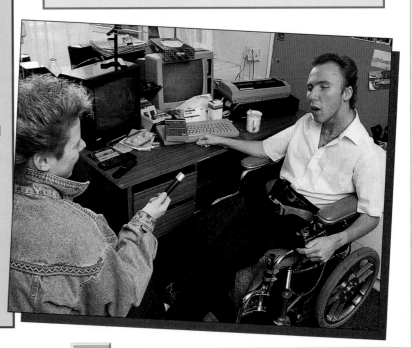

Dialects

A **dialect** is a type of English that is spoken by a particular group of people. A dialect has its own words and expressions and its own grammar rules. When a group of people from the same area speak the same dialect, it is called a **regional dialect**.

Today, many people throughout Britain speak the same type of English. Because it is used so widely, this dialect has become known as **Standard English**. It is the one used by news presenters and taught in schools.

Here is an example of two people speaking in a regional dialect:

Tina: I want some sarnies and a bevvy.

Jim: Well shift yourself, then.

Tina: I'll be back in a jiffy.

Jim: OK, then, I'll wait in the entry.

Here is the same conversation in Standard English:

Tina: I want some sandwiches and a drink.

Jim: Well hurry up, then.

Tina: I'll be back very quickly.

Jim: OK, then, I'll wait in the back alley.

Speaking, Listening and Writing

- In pairs, read the two versions of the conversation (above) out loud. Then make a list of the dialect words and expressions used in the first version and explain what each one means.

- Some words that you will hear used in American TV programmes sound strange, because American English is different from Standard English. Copy out this list and try to add some more.

American words	Standard English words
sidewalk	pavement
gas	petrol
garbage can	dustbin
fall	autumn

Here is another conversation in which the speakers are using a dialect.

Winston: It ain't right.

Leroy: We never done nothing.

Jasmin: We was sitting here, minding our own business.

Winston: Then them guys come over.

Jasmin: They start calling us names.

Winston: We ignoring them, like you told us.

Leroy: Then one of them pick up Jasmin's bag.

Winston: She tell him it hers. But he never take no notice.

Leroy: That what start it.

In this case, the speakers do not use any dialect words. But the dialect has different grammar rules from the grammar rules in Standard English.

Here is the same conversation in Standard English:

Winston: It isn't right.

Leroy: We didn't do anything.

Jasmin: We were sitting here, minding our own business.

Winston: Then those people came over.

Jasmin: They started calling us names.

Winston: We were ignoring them, like you told us to do.

Leroy: Then one of them picked up Jasmin's bag.

Winston: She told him it was hers, but he didn't take any notice.

Leroy: That's what started it.

In Groups

- Read the two conversations above.
- Pick out all the differences between the dialect version and the Standard English version.
- Make a list of all the changes.
- Talk about the grammatical reasons for the changes in a class discussion.

Glossary and Index

Accent Your accent is the way you pronounce words. *See page 93.*

Apostrophe The apostrophe is shaped like a comma. One of its uses is to show where a letter or letters have been missed out of a word, for example, as in 'don't'. *See page 49.*

Autobiography Writing your life story is called writing an autobiography. *See page 36.*

Capital letter A capital letter is a large letter used at the beginning of a sentence, and as the first letter of the names of people and places. *See pages 8–9.*

Cautionary tale A cautionary tale is a story that warns the reader not to do something. It explains what will happen to them if they ignore the warning. *See pages 84–85.*

Comic A comic is a magazine in which stories are told in pictures as well as in words. *See pages 16–19.*

Dialect A dialect is a type of English that is spoken by a particular group of people. *See pages 94–95.*

Draft A draft is a piece of writing that you are working on. *See page 36.*

Exclamation mark An exclamation mark is a punctuation mark which replaces a full stop to show that something dramatic is being said, for example, in 'Run quickly!' *See page 18.*

Full stop A full stop is a punctuation mark that comes at the end of the sentence. *See page 8.*

FX FX is an abbreviation used in radio scripts to mean 'sound effects'. *See page 88.*

Graphic novel A graphic novel is a book that looks like a comic, because it tells the story through pictures as well as words. *See pages 22–23.*

Legend A legend is an old story that was once believed to be true, but that is probably untrue. *See pages 60–69.*

Limerick A limerick is a five-line verse, made famous by a writer called Edward Lear. *See pages 56–57.*

List poem In a list poem, the writer develops his or her ideas in the form of a list. *See pages 52–54.*

Myth A myth is a story that was made up long ago, often to explain tha natural world and religious beliefs. *See pages 60–69.*

Noun A noun is any word that is the name of a thing, a person, a feeling or an idea. *See page 52.*

Paragraph A paragraph is a group of sentences, all of which are about the same idea or subject. *See pages 26–31.*

Plot The plot is the outline of the series of events that happen in a story. *See page 32.*

Plural The plural of a word is used to tell us that there is more than one of something. *See page 83.*

Question mark A question mark is a punctuation mark which replaces a full stop to show that a question is being asked, for example, 'What are you doing?' *See page 8.*

Recipe poem A recipe poem is a poem that is set out like the instructions for a recipe in a cookery book. *See page 55.*

Sentence A sentence is something written or spoken that makes sense. *See page 8.*

Shape poem A shape poem is one in which the words or lines of the poem are arranged to make a picture or shape. *See pages 50–51.*

Standard English Standard English is a common dialect of English, the one used by news presenters and taught in schools. *See page 94.*

Storyboard A storyboard is a series of pictures that show the main events of the plot. *See page 32.*

Verb A verb is a word that tells us what people or things are doing or being. *See page 53.*